Fresh & Honest

FOOD FROM THE FARMS OF NEW ENGLAND AND THE KITCHEN OF HENRIETTA'S TABLE

By Peter Davis

with Alexandra Hall

Photography by Heath Robbins

three
bean press

Fresh & Honest
Food From the Farms of New England and the Kitchen of Henrietta's Table
Published by:
Three Bean Press, LLC
P.O. Box 301711
Jamaica Plain, MA 02215
orders@threebeanpress.com • www.threebeanpress.com

Publishers Cataloging-in-Publication Data
Davis, Peter
Hall, Alexandra
Fresh & Honest: Food From the Farms of New England and the Kitchen of Henrietta's Table / by Peter Davis with Alexandra Hall; photography by Heath Robbins.
p. cm.
Summary: A cookbook of recipes from Chef Peter Davis' Cambridge, Mass., restaurant Henrietta's Table, highlighting New England cuisine and local purveyors.
ISBN 0-9767276-0-9
[1. Cookery. 2. New England. 3. Farms.] I. Robbins, Heath, Photographer. II. Title.
LCCN 2008908338

The Charles Hotel
One Bennett St.
Cambridge, MA 02138
800.882.1818
www.charleshotel.com

Printed in the U.S.A. on recycled paper.

Photos on previous pages: cover: Skillet Breakfast; inside cover: Massachusetts farmland; title page: Blue Cheese au Gratin Potatoes; opposite page: lobster traps, Nahant, Massachusetts. Inside back cover: Peter Davis fishing in Westport, Massachusetts.

Siena Farm,
Sudbury, Massachusetts

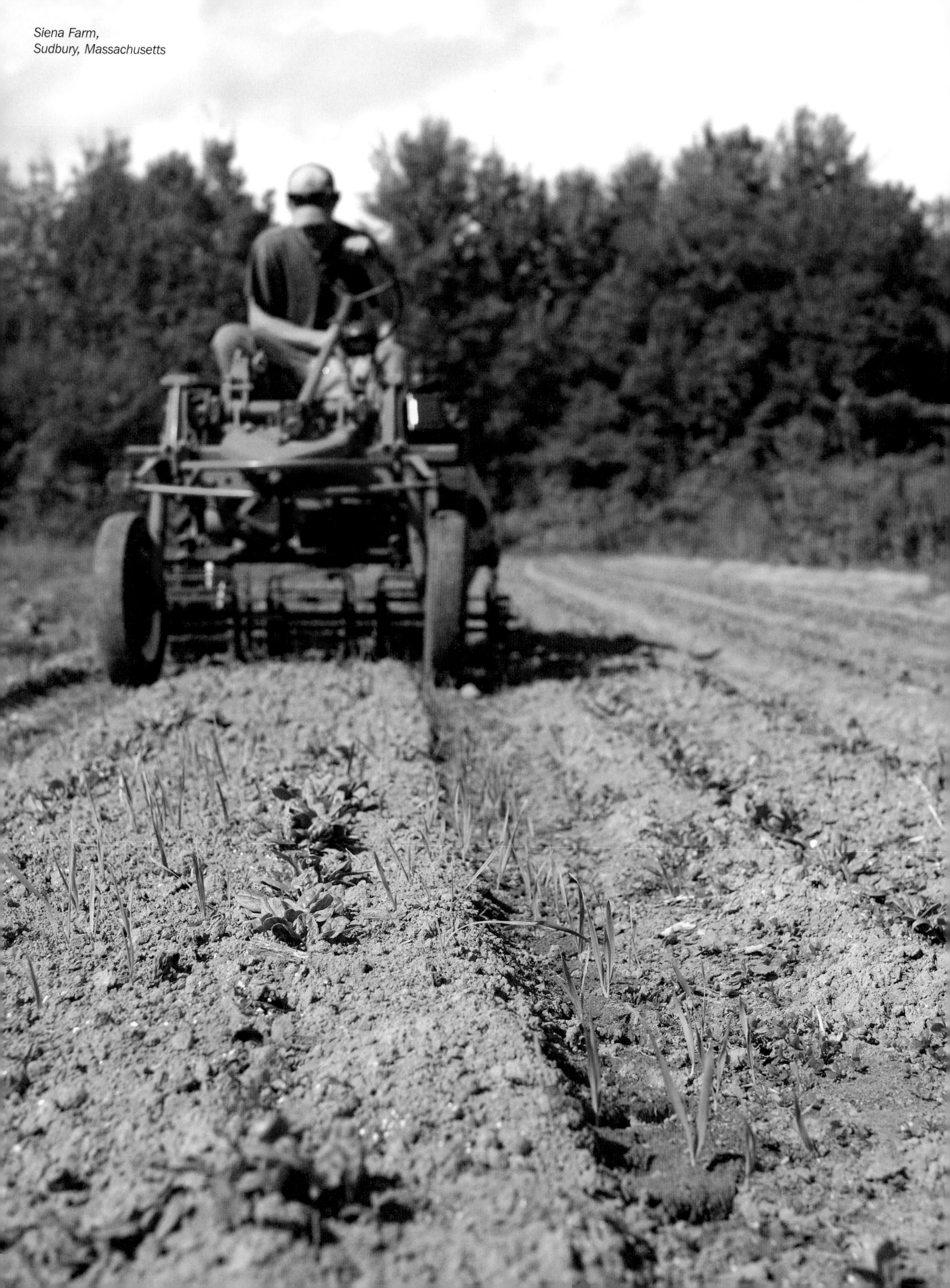

Fresh & Honest

This book is dedicated to:

My mother, who taught me to love food; to my father, whose work ethic inspired me; to my wife Peggy, daughter Jackie, and my son Sean, who have all patiently put up with me spending so much time at work over the years.

That work, meanwhile, was made notably more fulfilling by the creative hard work of all of my sous chefs, past and present, who have helped develop the restaurant and bring it to its full potential. That also includes Danny Angelopolus, my current pastry chef, who helped with all the recipes and pictures for the pastry chapter. I also need to thank the entire team—front and back of the house—of Henrietta's Table and The Charles Hotel. I undoubtedly owe a special debt of gratitude to Dick Friedman, who has inspired and challenged me to run the restaurant since even before its opening; and to writer Alexandra Hall, photographer Heath Robbins, food stylist Catrine Kelty, Three Bean Press, and The Charles Hotel. Without all of their support and hard work, this book could never have happened.

I also dedicate this book to all of the New England farms who contributed to it, and with whom we have worked so closely at the restaurant for so many wonderful and productive years. Those include, but aren't limited to, lobsterman Joel Marie, Chris Kurth at Siena Farm, Eero Ruuttila at Nesenkeag Co-op Farm, cheese maker Tricia Smith of Carlisle Farmstead, Steve Verrill at Verrill Farm, Pete Lowy and Jen Hashley at Pete and Jen's Backyard Birds, Eva Sommaripa at Eva's Garden, Pat Woodbury at Woodbury's Seafood, the Santo brothers at Shy Brothers Farm, Honey Pot Hill Orchards, Neil Couvee at Chippen Farm, Patti Powers at Cheshire Farm, Bob Stetson at Westfield Farm, Keith Martin at Elysian Fields Farm, lobsterman Ted Mahoney, Ron Konove at River Rock Farm, Tom Jurgielwicz at Jurgielwicz Farm, Tim Stone at Great Hill Blue Farm, Rob Litch at Misty Knoll Farm, and Pio Angelini at Angelini Farming Trust. What's more, I dedicate it to all of the small farms, fishermen, and aquaculturists across America. Their labors make cooking the best job I could ever have, and eating one of my life's greatest joys.

Biographies

Chef Peter Davis

Honored by The James Beard Foundation as one of "The Best Hotel Chefs in America," Executive Chef Peter Davis has created a popular, beloved culinary destination and a cult following with Henrietta's Table, located in The Charles Hotel, Harvard Square, Cambridge, Massachusetts. Named one of America's "Best Farm-to-Table" restaurants by *Gourmet* magazine, the eatery is a perfect complement to The Charles Hotel's hybrid culture of contemporary energy and awareness blended with traditional New England style.

Chef Davis, whose motto is "fresh and honest," as in "fresh from the farm and honest-to-goodness New England cooking," came to The Charles Hotel with impressive credentials from around the world. After working in highly-ranked international hotels including the Hyatt Regency Singapore, the Bali Hyatt, the Grand Hyatt Hong Kong, and The Peninsula Beverly Hills, he returned to his native city of Boston to become Executive Chef at The Charles Hotel in 1995. An avid conservationist with close ties to the fishing and farming communities of New England, Chef Davis was also one of the first proponents of local products. He will not use any genetically engineered foods or products at Henrietta's Table. A true "working chef," heavily involved in the daily operations of the restaurant, the opening of Henrietta's Table was a lifelong ambition.

Henrietta's Table features unpolished wood floors, mission-style chairs, an unpretentious ambiance, and a working market stocked with a mix of organic vegetables, fruits, and flowers at the entrance. The menu features daily and weekly specials, using the best of open market ingredients. Chef Davis uses organic and native ingredients from local producers throughout and beyond Massachusetts, creating an original and simple approach to classic New England cuisine. "Our main priority is the taste of the food," says Davis, "so we try not to put more than three or four ingredients on a plate." Davis' keen awareness of the integrity of food in its natural state, eye for color, and instinct for balance of tastes have earned him critical acclaim by *Travel & Leisure, USA Today,* and the Food Network.

Chef Davis is married with two children and currently lives close to the ocean in his native town of Nahant, Massachusetts.

About Alexandra Hall

Alexandra Hall has been a Boston-based food writer for more than 15 years, serving as a writer, editor, and critic for various food, travel, and lifestyle publications along the way. A graduate of Le Cordon Bleu culinary school in Paris, France, she has covered the dining scene in New England and beyond for publications including *Travel & Leisure, Food & Wine, The Boston Globe,* and *The New York Times.* She was a senior lifestyle editor and oversaw the food and dining section at *Boston Magazine* for four years, and is currently editor-in-chief of several lifestyle magazines produced by *The Boston Globe.* She writes regularly for *Bon Appétit* and *Town & Country Travel* magazines, and recently cowrote two guidebooks with her husband, Michael Blanding, *Moon New England* and *Moon Vermont.*

About Heath Robbins

An avid cook himself, Heath Robbins' passion for food is evident in his mouthwatering imagery. His pictures have graced the pages of national magazines such as *Bon Appétit, Food & Wine,* and *Gourmet* and can be seen in advertisements for Welch's Grape Jelly, Uncle Ben's and Sam's Club. Robbins recently photographed *The Korean Table,* a cookbook featuring easy to prepare Korean and Japanese recipes, as well as *Ciao Italia Big Five* for famed television host Mary Ann Esposito. Check out Robbins' blog at http://heathrobbins.blogspot.com to learn more about his current projects.

Table of Contents

Introduction	**10**
Growing Together: Henrietta's Table, The Big Pig Gig, and The Farm School	14
A Fresh Take	**18**
New England Seasonal Table	23
Breakfast & Brunch	**26**
Chippen Farm	33
Cheshire Garden	40
Soup & Salads	**44**
Nesenkeag Co-op Farm	51
Westfield Farm	57
Starters	**64**
Eva's Garden	75
Great Hill Blue Farm	80
Lunch & Dinner	**84**
Seafood	**86**
Ted Mahoney	91
Woodbury's Seafood	96
Meat	**102**
Elysian Fields Farm	109
River Rock Farm	117
Poultry	**122**
Misty Knoll Farm	124
Jurgielwicz Farm	132
Sides & Other Stuff	**134**
Angelini Farming Trust	159
Verrill Farm	169
Desserts & Drinks	**180**
Index	**208**

Introduction

Like all great culinary journeys, mine has been as much about finding my place in the world as it has been about finding my place in the kitchen. Whenever I have cooked and wherever I have eaten, the freshness of the food—and the directness of its journey from source to plate—has made all the difference in its flavor. Whether it's a tomato picked fresh from the vine or a lobster just caught at sea, my appreciation for how each ingredient grows has been cultivated throughout my childhood and in my travels to kitchens around the globe.

SEEDLING

I've always loved being outside—long before I ever picked up a pair of chef's knives. I grew up in Nahant, an isolated peninsula (Nahant means "almost an island" in Native American) on the North Shore of Boston, Massachusetts. It's an area teeming with rocky coasts, abundant fish, and equally abundant fishermen. As early as sixth grade, I realized I could turn my love of being outside into a job that fed people and made them happy. I bought my own boat—a used 16-foot Nova Scotia skiff with an old outboard motor—and every summer until I graduated from high school, I woke up just after sunrise, did my paper route, and set 20 to 25 lobster traps. I'd pull them up, heavy as they were and crammed with dripping crustaceans, and sell my catch to neighbors and friends. Sometimes I'd overhear rumors around town about where schools of mackerel could be found. I'd hop in my boat straightaway and chase them, catching as many as I could. Then I'd clean them on the picnic table

in our backyard with my dad's help. Afterward, I'd help my mom make dinner out of them; she was a traditional, easygoing cook. I loved watching her use the ingredients we found outdoors indoors, creating sweet-smelling dinners and pies.

As a kid, I was just as obsessed with the land as I was with the ocean. Our family "farm" was a big part of my responsibilities—whether it was weeding in the vegetable garden or tending the chickens. (Actually, I loved the chickens so much that when my dad threatened to get rid of them because they hadn't been laying eggs, I snuck store-bought eggs into their cages for him to find.) I remember how much better the tomatoes we grew tasted than any we ever bought—loads juicier, shouting sweet flavor, and still warm from the sun. It all taught me to respect the huge amount of work and time it takes to make things grow.

SPROUTING

The more I see of the earth, the more practicing my belief in sustainability and local dining becomes a reality. I first came face-to-face with the world's diversity of ingredients in my initial weeks of culinary school. I remember marveling at the quality, the colors, and the absolute freshness of everything that was brought in for us to cook with—from the spring lamb to bright-flavored, dark green arugula to white asparagus, a color I had never seen on stalks before.

But that was just a tiny taste of what I found later when working in some of the most vibrant, frenetic, and challenging kitchens of Asia—the Hyatt hotels in Singapore, Bali, and Hong Kong—then afterward, at the Peninsula Beverly Hills. At all of them, I cooked alongside incredibly skilled European and Asian chefs, but the availability of ingredients varied greatly.

In Bali, there were fresh genjer leaves to steam, long beans to marinate, and jackfruit to simmer in coconut milk. But certain essentials simply weren't available. In fact, there was such a dearth of basic supplies, several other chefs and I snuck seeds for beans and herbs into

the country to give to local farmers. We essentially created a collaborative underground—a boon to the farmers, who suddenly found themselves growing things they'd never seen before, and reaping an additional source of income. Local purveyors who you can count on are always preferable—that's a lesson I still keep in mind with every menu I plan.

In Hong Kong, I worked with a Chinese chef who taught me how to assess the freshness of fish (cut into the flesh to make sure the fishmonger didn't just wash the outside to make it look fresh) and tricks to preserve food so we could have great tastes year-round. Everything we

did in that kitchen was about the intensity of flavor. We used high-heat sautéing to lock in the flavors with an unbelievably hot sear, and used high, hot flames to get as much flavor from the wok as possible.

Later I had a very different—and eye-opening— experience during a stint in China; because the government controlled everything, you were never sure what kind of ingredients you'd receive. Planning a menu was an impossibility, so I learned to cook on the fly. If they only sent me potatoes and carrots, I'd have to dig up four ways to cook carrots and four ways to cook potatoes.

This was in stark contrast to my time in Los Angeles at The Peninsula Beverly Hills; the quality of seafood and produce was nothing short of amazing. We had everything we needed, 12 months a year. The fusion trend was just starting to gain steam at that time, and my restaurant chef was French-trained Japanese, so we made a lot of East-meets-West menus. That meant we were getting a full roster of diverse, simply incredible foods, and with every dish, I got to hone and solidify my philosophy: The closer from wok to mouth, the better.

That's a practice I still hold dear; I like my food hot, fresh, and served immediately. No sitting around on a steam table—if I stir-fry chili crab, I walk it right out so it can be eaten immediately. I also like simple, pure flavors that sing. That's the obsession in Asia, and in fact, in all the places I've worked: Get it as fresh as possible, cook it, and get it to the table, pronto.

RIPE FOR THE PICKING

The "back to the land" philosophy is precisely what spurred us to open Henrietta's Table in 1995—long before organic foods became trendy, I should add. Since opening The Charles Hotel a decade earlier, owner Dick Friedman had made the place an institution in Harvard Square, Cambridge. (For hard-core devotees, it's second only in stature to Harvard University itself!) The hotel earned its following by seamlessly bringing together

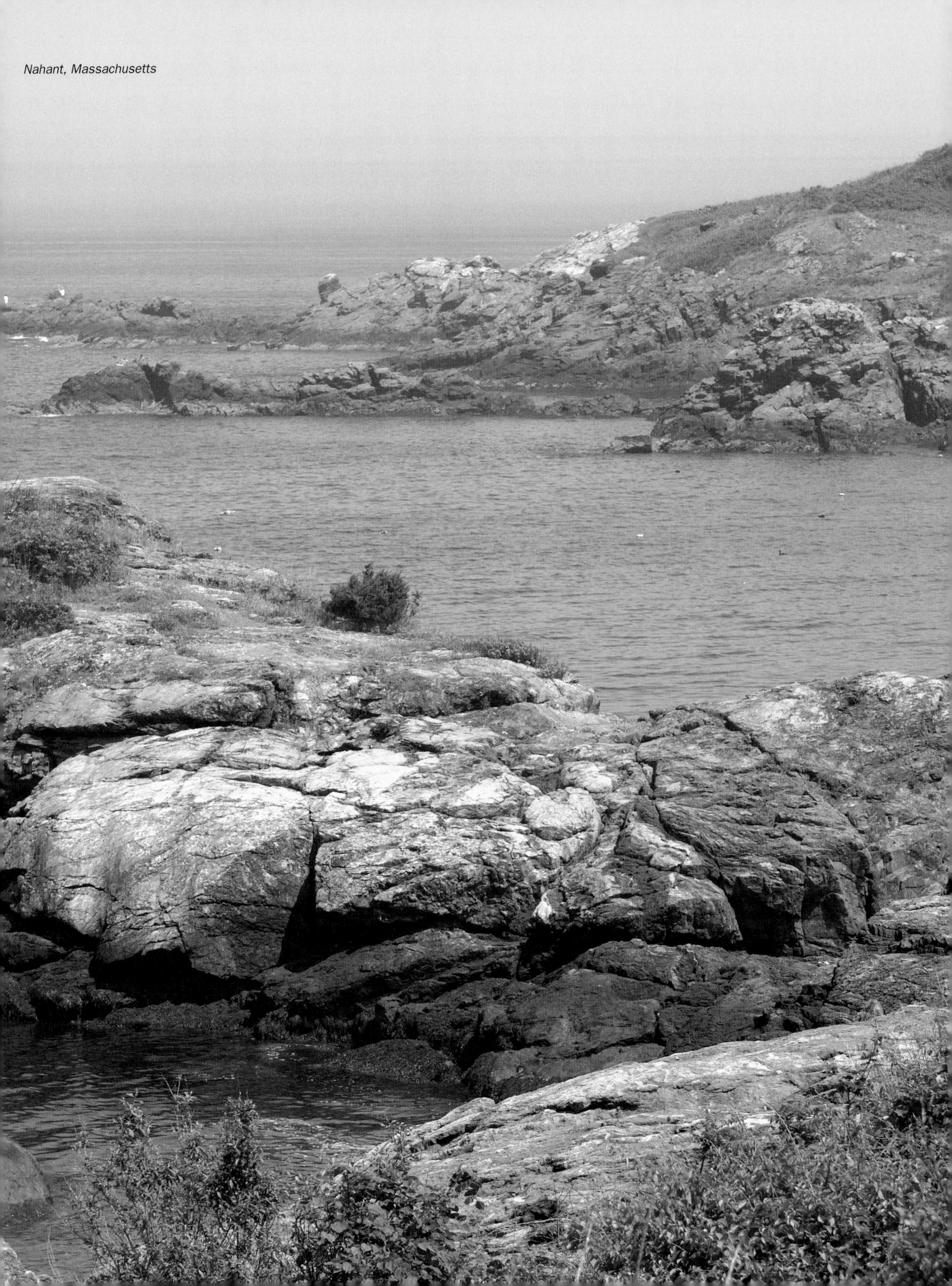

Nahant, Massachusetts

Growing Together: Henrietta's Table, The Big Pig Gig, and The Farm School

The Farm School was started in 1989 with a simple goal: to give children the same direct experience of farming that founder Ben Holmes had been given while growing up on his family farm. Just as he was handed a bucket and asked to help feed the calves from an early age, Holmes wanted to pass along what it feels like to take care of something other than yourself—a lesson that's arguably even harder these days, given how current generations have been so removed from contact with the environment and living world.

The very simplicity and consistency of The Farm School's intention is one of the reasons why it has been so successful. The place serves over 1,700 children each year in immersive, three-day programs and now also includes a year-long farmer training program for adults and a full-time middle school. Every day The Farm School does just what it sets out to do: It hands that proverbial (and literal) bucket over, and helps children and adults make a meaningful and measurable contribution to the work of the farm, and to become inexorably connected to the earth and to something deep within themselves.

Henrietta's Table couldn't be more proud to support The Farm School in the ways that we do. For the past six years, we've hosted an annual fund-raising event, The Big Pig Gig, as a gift to the School that provides it with the funds to continue. It's also an incredibly fun and gratifying night, with three distinct parts: an elegant dinner for 400 guests, an auction that raises hundreds of thousands of dollars (in particular to support scholarships), and a musical performance by a renowned performer (past years have seen artists such as Bob Weir and Mavis Staples).

The event works, and works incredibly well, because the fit between Henrietta's Table and The Farm School is so natural. Every day at the restaurant we set out to serve food that celebrates its source, and the vital relationships we have with those who grow it. We couldn't think of a better partner than The Farm School, or a more delicious cause to share with all the dedicated people who help us support the School.

Verrill Farm's freshly picked tomatoes

classic New England design sensibility and luxurious amenities and services. It stood to reason that Friedman was looking to open the restaurant equivalent of that within the hotel—a simple, unpretentious eatery serving impeccable dishes full of New England ingredients.

Our visions meshed the minute we started talking. We decided to name the endeavor Henrietta's Table, after Dick's late pig. We would serve food fresh from farm to table, with a core of unchanging classics on the menu (everything from Roasted Corn and Crab Chowder with smoked bacon to the Cornmeal-Crusted Monkfish Sandwich dolloped with house-made Tartar Sauce), plus a wide array of market-dependent specials.

The specials are paramount at the restaurant—and to me. That's where my love of freshness truly shines, because they are dictated by only the most extraordinary products the farmers have to offer that day. I'm on the phone with them constantly—so often that many have become personal friends—discussing which crops look most promising this week, what they're getting excited about around the bend, and planning my menus based on what they tell me.

I also visit all the farmers once or twice a year, spending plenty of time with folks like Steve Verrill of Verrill Farm, Eero Ruuttila at Nesenkeag Co-op Farm, and my many favorite cheese makers in Vermont. They know that the restaurant and I are as dedicated to sustainable agriculture and native ingredients as they are, and they also know about our longtime support of The Farm School (see sidebar, page 14). Just as importantly,

though, the farms we work with know and trust that we'll cook and serve what they send us in a way that will enhance—not disguise—the beautiful natural flavor.

Honoring the source is what every culinary experience I've ever had, from lobstering as a child to bean smuggling in Bali, has led up to. It's what the food at Henrietta's Table is about. And it's carried through in all of the recipes that follow. Each dish is a culmination of the culinary journey I have taken over the years. And each one is meant to respect the food's own journey from its source to your table. I hope these recipes will become an indispensable part of your own culinary journey, and that they are as much fun to eat as they are to make. Dig in!

Joel Marie lobstering off of Nahant, Massachusetts

A Fresh Take

The recipes in this book don't depend on fancy cooking techniques, heavy and overwrought sauces, or ingredients so rare you've never heard of them. Instead they get their flavor from the food itself. That flavor depends on how the food was treated from the moment it first started growing until the moment it lands on your kitchen counter. To get the most from the following recipes, make sure the ingredients you use to prepare them are as fresh and honest as they can be. Do it for the sake of your palate, your health, and the earth from which they came.

You'll want to know precisely where your food is grown, and get it as locally as you can. For that reason, instead of listing specific New England resources, farms, and purveyors (although you'll find a few peppered throughout this book), I recommend you seek sources that offer sustainable, responsible, and flavorful foods that are close to your home. It pays to go straight to the farm (or as close to it as humanly possible), and to pay attention, not only to what you buy, but to how you buy it. From finding organic farms and free-range meats to getting downright finicky—inspecting, poking, and sniffing—when selecting your produce, the following tips and practices will make all the difference in the quality, the sustainability, and, ultimately, the taste of everything you eat.

Here you'll find some essential tips that we use at Henrietta's Table when choosing produce, meats, poultry, and seafood from our New England suppliers. The list isn't meant to be comprehensive—just things to look for when buying food from a farmers' market.

Produce

I can't say it enough: Buy local, local, local. Not only will your fruits and vegetables be fresher, you'll also be lowering your carbon impact; Local produce hasn't been trucked across the country and hasn't caused exhaust pollution and fuel consumption in the process. Farmers' markets are by far the best way to get to know local farmers. Find favorites in your area and visit them regularly. Most importantly, form relationships with the farmers you buy from.

Even when you aren't buying local, research where your food is from and make sure you know how it's grown. Look for farms that grow organically or pledge low-pesticide management. (Though, don't assume that something that's labeled organic is necessarily sustainably or responsibly raised. When you decide where to buy your foods, get as educated about your source as possible. Learn as much as you can, and form your own judgments.) This will leave your body as chemical-free as possible, the earth a cleaner place, and your produce tasting pure and true to its real flavor.

Whenever possible, buy what's in season. In New England, that means looking for berries in the summertime, corn and tomatoes in mid- and late-summer, and apples and squash in the fall. (A seasonal buying guide for New England follows.) Then, without question, eat it all as soon as you can get it to your table.

Fruits

Apples should have tight skin, be firm when gently pressed, and be free of bruises or punctures.

Berries ought to have no mold or oozing juices and should smell fresh.

Look for melons that are heavy in weight, have a fresh smell and a slight give on the non-stem end.

Pears, even when firm, should have a slight give when pressed.

Stone fruits (meaning fruits with pits, like peaches, plums, and cherries) should have a good fragrant smell, tight skin, be free of bruises, and have a slight give when gently pressed.

Vegetables

Asparagus should be bright green, with firm stalks, and tight skin, and is best in spring.

Broccoli and cauliflower should be fresh-looking and firm to the touch. The tops should not be flowering.

Corn tastes best if bought and eaten the same day it was picked; it loses flavor quickly. Buy those with tight, bright husks, soft and light brown silk, and shiny, plump kernels.

Cucumbers ought to be firm, unwaxed, and four to six inches long.

Lettuce, salad, and cooking greens should be checked thoroughly to make sure they have no wilting, and aren't dry, yellowed, or mushy. If you're buying mixed greens, open up the leaves and check them individually.

Pole beans (those beans grown on a pole—such as green beans and their multicolored cousins) should be brightly hued, firm (with no hollow feeling), and have a good snap, with small beans inside.

For potatoes, root vegetables (turnips, yams, carrots, parsnips), onions, or anything else grown underground, look for firmness. If the greens are attached, check them to see if they are fresh or old and wilted. Potatoes should have no green skins, sproutings, or mold.

Harvesting clams at Woodbury's Seafood

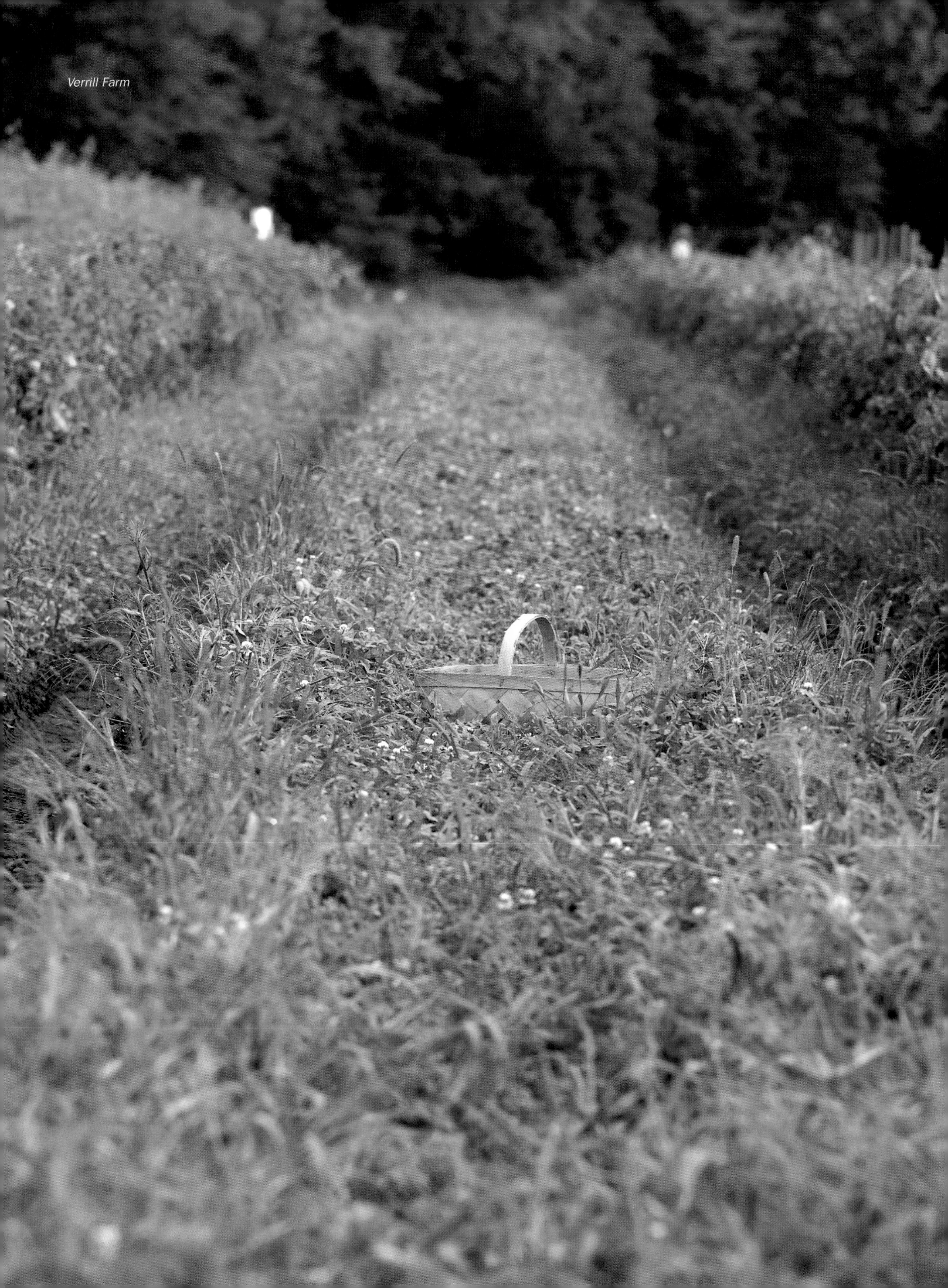

Verrill Farm

New England Seasonal Table

	April	May	June	July	August	September	October	November	December
Acorn Squash						x	x	x	x
Apple Cider					x	x	x	x	x
Apples					x	x	x	x	x
Arugula	x	x	x	x	x				
Asparagus		x	x						
Beans			x	x	x	x	x		
Beets			x	x	x	x	x	x	x
Blackberries					x	x			
Blueberries					x	x			
Bok Choy		x	x	x	x				
Broccoli		x				x			
Broccoli Rabe		x		x		x	x		
Brussels Sprouts						x	x		
Butternut Squash						x	x	x	x
Cabbage			x	x	x	x	x	?	
Carrots					x	x	x	x	
Cauliflower				x		x			
Chard			x	x	x	x	x	x	
Collard Greens			x	x	x	x			
Corn				x	x				
Cucumbers				x	x	x			
Eggplant						x	x		
Endive					x	x	x		
English Peas			x						
Fennel		x		x	x				
Fiddleheads	x	x							
Grapes						x	x		
Heirloom Winter Squashes						x	x	x	x
Herbs		x	x	x	x	x	x		
Hot Peppers			x	x	x	x			
Kohlrabi		x	x	x	x	x	x	x	
Lettuces		?	x	x	x	x	x	?	
Onions						x	x	x	
Onions - bunching				x	x				
Onions - green (scallion)		x	x	x					
Onions - sweet						x	x	x	
Parsnips	x	x				x	x	x	
Pea Greens	x	x	x	x					
Peaches and Nectarines					x	x			
Pears						x	x		
Peas			x	x					
Plums				x	x	x			
Potatoes						x	x	x	x
Potatoes - fingerling				x	x	x	x	x	x
Potatoes - new			x	x	x	x	x	x	x
Pumpkins						x	x	x	
Radicchio				x	x	x			
Radishes		x	x	x	x	x			
Ramps	x	x							
Raspberries					x	x			
Rhubarb		x	x	x	x	x			
Rutabagas						x	x		
Shell Beans							x	x	
Snap Peas		x	x						
Snow Peas			x						
Spinach		x	x			x	x		
Strawberries			x	x					
Summer Squashes			x	x	x	x			
Sweet Peppers					x	x			
Tomatoes - cherry			x	x	x	x	x		
Tomatoes - heirloom				x	x	x			
Tomatoes - plum				x	x	x	x		
Tomatoes - round				x	x	x	x		
Turnips - Hakurei			x	x	x	x	x		
Turnips - Macomber						x	x	x	x
Turnips - purple top					x	x	x	x	
Zucchini			x	x	x	x			

x= in season • ?=depending on weather

Rhubarb should be bright, shiny, and snap when it's bent.

Shell beans (those beans grown and eaten for their edible seed rather than their pod—cranberry beans are a popular type) are best when they have tough pods, without any yellowing, and firm beans inside.

Choose summer squashes that are small to medium in size, are semi-firm, and have smooth, shiny skin. Winter or hard-skin squashes should be firm, not bruised, and with no mold around the stems.

Meat and Poultry

Look for beef, pork, and lamb that have been raised in a pasture and fed grass their entire lives. Chicken and poultry should be free-range (i.e. cage-free) and not feed lot–raised. This results in better flavor and texture, and also greatly increases the odds that the livestock has

been raised without cruelty. To this end, search out meat and poultry that have been given no hormones, steroids, or growth additives. This ensures better lives for them, and cleaner, better-tasting food for you. Be sure to sniff everything before you buy. Everything should have a good, fresh scent, a bright color (not hazy), be firm to the touch, and should never be slimy or mushy.

Choose eggs that are cage-free, ideally local, and from chickens that have not been fed any unnatural foods or hormones. Brown or white really doesn't matter in flavor or quality.

Seafood

Buy from fish markets, and get to know your purveyor. Ask where the fish is from and when it was caught. Anything with a face should have bright, clear eyes and

the flesh should have a firm texture, and a sharp, not hazy, color. If you bend the fish slightly, its meat should adhere to the spine—meat that pulls off isn't fresh.

Clams, oysters, and mussels should have closed shells, smell like the sea, and be free of any slime.

When buying scallops, look for dry-packed, which means they haven't been soaked in a brine solution to preserve them. They should be slightly shiny, off-white, and slightly opaque in color, and with a light seafood odor.

When buying lobster or crab, check for liveliness. This is a good indication of freshness. When buying cooked crustaceans, look for meat that's firm, not slimy, and has a fresh smell.

If fresh fish isn't available, buy only the kind that's labeled and sold as 'frozen at sea.' This means it was frozen soon after it was caught, as opposed to being frozen much later.

Look for shrimp that are fresh, wild-caught, or sustainably farmed. Color and type vary with each kind of shrimp and size, but all should have a clear shell and fresh smell.

If the fish has been farmed, find out where, since many farms right now raise fish in a way that pollutes or destroys the environment. So by all means, ask if the farm is sustainable. (Find out more about seafood sustainability in your specific area on the terrific Web site for The Monterey Bay Aquarium: www. montereybayaquarium.org/cr/seafoodwatch.asp.)

*Early morning
watering at Eva's*

Breakfast & Brunch

Pete and Jen's Backyard Birds

You know what they say: Breakfast is the most important meal of the day. And it is. But when we serve it at Henrietta's Table it's also one of our most personal meals of the day. It's when we catch up with so many of our regulars, who come in for everything from flavor-layered dishes like Red Flannel Hash with Poached Eggs to Cinnamon-Cranberry French Toast to simple specialties like our house-made granola. Every weekend, we make a big deal out of brunch, with a huge buffet that brings in swarms of families, many of whom have made it a weekly ritual for years. Don't be surprised if the following recipes become rituals in your home, too; like everything on our menu, they're relatively easy to make, and rely far less on fanciness than on freshness and pure flavor.

Baked Strawberry Rhubarb French Toast

Serves 4

Ingredients:

For the batter:

2 eggs

½ teaspoon cinnamon

⅛ teaspoon nutmeg

½ pint milk

1 tablespoon vanilla

½ cup heavy cream

For the French toast:

8 slices challah bread

1 cup strawberry rhubarb jam

½ cup heavy cream

½ cup maple syrup

Directions:

To make the batter:

Mix the eggs, cinnamon, and nutmeg in a large bowl, then whisk in the milk, vanilla, and cream until everything is incorporated.

To make the French toast:

Spread the bread with the jam and arrange shingle-style in an ovenproof casserole dish. Pour the French toast batter over the top and gently move the bread so the batter surrounds it.

Refrigerate the mix overnight.

Preheat oven to 350 degrees.

Cover the French toast casserole and bake to an internal temperature of 165 degrees (approximately 30 minutes).

In a medium bowl, whip the heavy cream with a whisk or beater.

Remove the casserole cover and brown lightly, about 15 minutes.

Remove from the oven and serve with the whipped cream and maple syrup.

Cinnamon-Cranberry French Toast

Serves 4

Ingredients:

For the French toast:

½ cup dried cranberries

1 cup maple syrup

2 ounces butter

8 slices cinnamon raisin bread

For the batter:

2 eggs

½ teaspoon cinnamon

¾ pint of milk

⅛ teaspoon nutmeg

1 tablespoon vanilla

½ cup heavy cream

Directions:

Marinate the cranberries in the maple syrup for 2 hours (can be done up to 2 days before).

To make the batter: Mix the eggs and cinnamon in a large bowl, then whisk in the milk, nutmeg, vanilla, and cream until everything is incorporated.

To make the French toast: Melt half of the butter in a nonstick skillet or pan.

In a separate saucepan, set the cranberry-syrup mixture on low heat to warm.

Dip the bread into the batter and coat on both sides.

Brown both sides of the French toast, pour the warm syrup over it, and serve with the remaining butter.

Whole Wheat Hotcakes

Serves 6 to 8

Ingredients:

1 pound whole wheat flour, sifted

½ teaspoon baking powder

1 teaspoon baking soda

1 teaspoon salt

3 eggs

3 egg whites

4 tablespoons honey

1½ pints milk

4 tablespoons safflower oil

Directions:

Sift dry ingredients into a large bowl. Mix in the eggs, egg whites, honey, milk, and oil and stir until just blended.

Cook over medium heat in a nonstick pan or on a greased griddle. Flip when small bubbles appear at the surface. Serve with maple syrup and butter.

Grilled Vegetables with Chèvre and Basil Oil

Serves 6

I love this salad. The mellow sweetness of the herb-infused marinade is a perfect match for the tartness of the goat cheese. And, with the grilled vegetables added in, the entire thing makes for a deeply flavored but simple salad. It's terrific served hot off the grill, or cold.

Ingredients:

For the marinade:

2 cups extra virgin olive oil

3 tablespoons chives, chopped

4 cloves garlic, chopped

3 tablespoons parsley, chopped

4 shallots, chopped

1 tablespoon rosemary, chopped

1 tablespoon thyme, chopped

For the vegetables:

1 zucchini

1 summer squash

1 carrot

1 eggplant

5 plum tomatoes, halved

2 red onions, small to medium in size

Kosher salt to taste

3 teaspoons freshly ground black pepper

1 small block goat cheese (4 oz.)

Basil oil to taste

Directions:

Combine all marinade ingredients in a deep-sided bowl and whisk thoroughly. Set aside.

Slice all vegetables about ¼-inch in diameter. Place in a large pan and cover with marinade. Cover tightly with plastic wrap and set aside for 30-35 minutes in a cool place. Do not refrigerate.

Drain the marinade from the vegetables, season with salt and pepper, and grill over medium heat, being careful not to let any burn.

Arrange the vegetables on a platter, sprinkle with crumbled goat cheese, and drizzle with basil oil. Serve.

Duck Hash

Serves 4

Ingredients:

8 ounces duck meat, cooked

½ cup red onion, diced

½ cup red, green, and yellow bell peppers, diced

4 cup olive oil

1 cup potato, cooked and diced

2 tablespoons white vinegar

8 eggs

Directions:

Cut the duck meat into thin strips.

In a heavy-bottomed pan, sauté the onion and peppers in the oil until the onion is transparent. Add the potatoes and duck, and sauté until golden brown.

Fill a separate pot a quarter of the way with water and add vinegar. Bring to a simmer and poach the eggs.

Arrange the hash mix onto 4 plates and top with 2 poached eggs each.

Fondue

Serves 4

*Fondue may not exactly be standard brunch fare in your house,
but I guarantee that after serving it once, it will be.*

Ingredients:

½ pound Gruyère cheese, coarsely grated

½ pound Emmenthaler cheese, coarsely grated

6 teaspoons cornstarch

1 clove garlic, peeled

1¾ cups Pinot gris

3 tablespoons Kirshwasser

A pinch of nutmeg

White pepper

One loaf French bread, cubed

Directions:

Toss the cheeses with the cornstarch.

Rub the sides of a fondue pot with the garlic clove. Pour the Pinot gris into the pot and cook over medium heat, until the wine comes to a simmer. Add the grated cheeses and stir until the cheese is incorporated.

Stir the Kirshwasser into the cheese and bring mixture to a boil. Remove from the heat and place in a fondue holder.

Season with nutmeg and pepper.

Serve with cubed bread to dip into the cheese.

Chippen Farm
Bedford, Massachusetts

Name: Neil Couvee

What I make: Farm-fresh eggs.

How I make it: We use floor and nest birds, so they get sunlight, they get humanely treated, and are given pure feed with no antibiotics or additives.

My average day: We collect eggs three times a day, and then we wash and grade them every day, so they can be sold as fresh as possible.

What makes us special: Our eggs are natural and fresh, and taste better for it. We also have a full-service stand where you can get eggs that have just been collected.

How to use them in the kitchen: In your favorite dish that calls for eggs, as you would any other. But these will have more flavor, and you'll know they're all-natural.

H.T. Granola

Makes 3 quarts

Ingredients:

5 cups bran

9 cups oats

¾ cup slivered almonds

¾ cup hazelnuts

¼ cup pumpkin seeds

¾ cup sunflower seeds

½ teaspoon salt

4 tablespoons cinnamon

1½ tablespoons vanilla

¾ cup maple sugar

2 cups firmly packed brown sugar

1½ cups molasses

1½ cups wheat germ

4 cups clarified butter

Directions:

Preheat oven to 325 degrees.

Mix all ingredients together and combine evenly.

Divide and spread onto 3 roasting pans no more than 1-inch high.

Place in the oven for approximately 30 to 40 minutes, taking time every 10 minutes to stir the granola around a bit to make sure it browns evenly.

Remove from oven when the nuts are light golden brown and the mixture is dry.

Cool and store in an airtight container at room temperature.

It is best served with fresh fruit and yogurt.

Poached Salmon with Cucumber Dill Crème Fraîche

Serves 6

Ingredients:

2 cucumbers

1 lemon

½ teaspoon peppercorns

⅛ cup onion, chopped

⅛ cup parsley, chopped

6 6-ounce salmon filets, skin removed

2 tablespoons fresh dill, chopped

1 cup crème fraîche

2 tablespoons fresh lemon juice

Salt and pepper

1 head bibb lettuce

12 cherry tomatoes

Directions:

Peel, seed, and dice the cucumbers and set aside.

Fill a saucepan one-third of the way with water and season with a squeeze of lemon, peppercorns, onion, and parsley. Bring to a simmer and poach the salmon until just cooked through (approximately 5 minutes).

Remove from the poaching liquid to cool.

Mix the cucumber, dill, crème fraîche, and lemon juice, and season with salt and pepper.

Wash the lettuce and arrange on a platter. Top with the salmon and cucumber mixture. Garnish with the tomatoes and serve.

Red Flannel Hash with Poached Eggs

Serves 6

This is a traditional New England dish, and a crafty way to use leftovers—making them taste completely new with the addition of beets. I like to serve this hearty dish with hollandaise sauce, but it's also rich enough to stand on its own. Feel free to substitute the raw brisket for cooked corned beef.

Ingredients:

2 pounds red corned beef brisket

½ cup parsnips

½ cup carrots

½ cup onions

½ cup potatoes, peeled

½ cup rutabagas, peeled

½ cup turnips

½ cup beets, peeled

2 tablespoons white vinegar

12 eggs

Directions:

Boil corned beef until tender. Strain corned beef and cool.

In the same pot, boil all vegetables except for the beets for 10 to 15 minutes until all are just fork-tender, being careful not to overcook.

Boil beets separately, also until just tender.

Strain and chop all vegetables into several pieces each.

Run the meat through a meat grinder by hand. Run the vegetables through the grinder. In a large bowl, mix meat and vegetables together.

Fill a separate pot one-quarter of the way with water and add vinegar. Bring to a simmer and poach the eggs.

While eggs are cooking, transfer the hash mixture to a skillet and sauté until golden brown. Then flip and brown other side.

Divide hash among 6 plates. Top with 2 eggs each and serve.

Scotch Eggs

Serves 6

Ingredients:

10 eggs

12 ounces ground
sausage meat

1 cup all-purpose flour

1 cup fine bread crumbs

2 cups canola oil

6 cups mixed field greens

12 cherry tomatoes,
sliced in half

½ cup Mustard Vinaigrette
(see page 175)

Directions:

Hard-boil 6 of the eggs. Peel and set aside to cool.

Place the sausage meat between 2 sheets of plastic wrap, and roll it out to a ¼-inch thickness using a rolling pin. Cut the meat into 6 equal squares.

Wrap each sausage square around each one of the boiled eggs, pressing where necessary to completely and evenly cover the egg.

Crack the remaining eggs into a bowl and whisk together. Dip the sausage-coated eggs into the flour, then into the whisked eggs, and roll in the bread crumbs to coat.

In a large saucepan, heat the oil to 375 degrees.

Fry the eggs in the oil until golden brown, about 5 minutes. Remove from the oil and drain.

Arrange the greens and tomatoes evenly on 6 plates, cut the eggs in half, and drizzle with the Mustard Vinaigrette just before serving.

Cheshire Garden, Winchester, New Hampshire

Name: Patti Powers

What I make: Preserves, mustards, sauces, and vinegars—all handmade from the bounty of our small farm.

How I got started: I've been gardening all my life, and began farming in earnest 30 years ago on a small farm in western Massachusetts. In 1986, I joined Cheshire Garden. Berries are our passion, and we've carved terraces into the hillside to create beds for raspberries, strawberries, blueberries, blackberries, currants, and elderberries, plus tomatoes and herbs. We have a small orchard of a couple dozen Damson plums, Seckel pears, and peaches, too.

How everything is made: We pick all of our fruit when it's fully ripe and all its flavor notes are expressed. We make our preserves the old-fashioned way: by boiling the fruit in a wide kettle with just enough sugar to ensure a soft set. I stir each kettle of boiling fruit as it cooks down. When the preserves thicken, I begin testing each batch by coating and tilting the spoon until the mixture falls away in a sheet. Then I fill each jar and my partner Ralph covers and cans them. Each kettle makes just a dozen jars.

What's special about what we do: Our preserves have a deeper color, more intense flavor, and softer texture than ordinary jams. Since we don't rely on pectin to facilitate a quick set, we can use less sugar than most jams.

How to use them in the kitchen: Our soft-set preserves spread easily over scones, muffins, toast, and any breakfast bread. They are also wonderful with desserts like trifles, cheesecakes, and tarts. Their intense flavors make them fun to experiment with in glazes or sauces for meat, poultry, and seafood. At Henrietta's Table, Peter features them on his cheese plates.

My favorite way to eat it all: On cold winter days, I really appreciate the fruits' brightness on scones or waffles or in bread pudding. In spring, when the first fresh eggs are available, I love to make crepes and fill them with preserves and yogurt.

Butternut Squash Pie

Serves 8 to 10

Ingredients:

2 butternut squashes

2 eggs

2 egg yolks

1 cup heavy cream

½ teaspoon cinnamon

½ teaspoon nutmeg

½ teaspoon allspice

Salt and pepper to taste

1 prebaked 8-inch pie round

Directions:

Preheat oven to 350 degrees.

Cut squashes in half and remove seeds. Place on a sheet tray in the oven for approximately 45 minutes or until squash is tender. Remove squash meat from the skin and puree. Set aside to cool.

In a large bowl, mix the eggs with the yolks, cream, and spices, and fold in the cooled squash.

Season with salt and pepper and place in the baked pie round. Bake at 350 degrees for 45 minutes, or until the pie sets.

Remove from the oven and serve warm.

Creamed Chipped Beef on Buttermilk Biscuits

Serves 4

For this recipe, you can use good-quality store-bought buttermilk biscuits or your favorite homemade version—both work well. One element I refuse to cut corners on, however, is the pepper: Make sure it's straight from the mill. I promise it will make all the difference.

Ingredients:

6 ounces chipped beef

4 cups heavy cream

Cracked black pepper

4 Buttermilk Biscuits (see page 149)

4 tablespoons chives, chopped

Directions:

In a saucepan, heat the beef and cream and simmer until the cream thickens. Season with pepper to taste.

Break the biscuits in half and toast.

Place the biscuits on a plate, pour the beef mixture over, and sprinkle with the chives.

Skillet Breakfast

Serves 4

I like to serve this breakfast in individually-sized cast-iron skillets, straight out of the oven. But if you don't happen to have any, it certainly tastes just as good off a regular dinner plate.

Ingredients:

4 medium-sized potatoes or 2 large ones

8 breakfast sausages

8 slices bacon

2 tablespoons butter

8 eggs

½ cup cheddar cheese, shredded

Salt and pepper to taste

Directions:

Preheat oven to 350 degrees.

Peel and boil the potatoes until fork-tender. Shred or grate them until you have 2 cups' worth.

Bring the sausage to a boil in water. Drain and cool.

Cook the bacon until halfway done.

Lightly brown the potato in butter.

In a small skillet, arrange 2 pieces of sausage, 2 pieces of bacon, ½ cup of potato, and crack 2 eggs into the pan. Sprinkle with the cheese. Repeat in 3 more skillets.

Bake for 20 minutes or until the eggs are cooked. Season with salt and pepper and serve immediately.

Soup & Salads

LOOSE
BOLERO
CARROTS
$2.00/lb

I tend to think of soups and salads as the yin and yang of how to begin a meal: The former is about the interplay of mellowed flavors and soul-warming satisfaction; the latter celebrates direct flavor, raw freshness, and incredible texture. In both cases here, I've chosen my favorite examples of homey and nourishing recipes—the ones our customers have asked for time and time again, and the ones I've tweaked with new ingredients and improved over the years. As with all of the food in this book, local ingredients make an enormous difference in the end result—but even more so in salads, where your resourcefulness and meticulousness in finding great-quality ingredients can start the entire meal on a high note.

Roasted Corn and Crab Chowder

Serves 8

Ingredients:

4 ears corn, unhusked

½ gallon Chicken Stock (see page 163)

2 strips bacon, diced

½ cup onion, diced

½ cup celery, diced

3 tablespoons all-purpose flour

6 medium-sized new potatoes, cut into bite-sized cubes

½ teaspoon ground turmeric

½ pound rock crabmeat

Salt and pepper to taste

Directions:

Preheat oven to 450 degrees. Bake the corn in their husks for 40 minutes. Remove from the oven and cool.

Husk the corn and remove the kernels with a knife. Set aside.

Take ½ cup of the stock and bring to a boil in a saucepan. Add three-quarters of the corn kernels and cook on medium heat for 20 minutes. Puree the mixture in a blender or food processor.

In a large pot, sauté the bacon until lightly browned. Add the onion and celery and cook until transparent. Add the flour and cook over low heat for 20 minutes, stirring to keep from burning.

Gradually add the potatoes and remaining stock. Cover and cook until the potatoes are soft. Add the corn puree, reserved kernels, turmeric, and crabmeat.

Cook on medium heat for 10 minutes. Season with salt and pepper and serve.

Chicken Noodle Soup

Serves 8

Ingredients:

1 cup celery, diced

1 cup onion, diced

1 cup carrot, diced

2 tablespoons olive oil

½ gallon Chicken Stock (see page 163)

2 cups chicken meat, cooked and diced

1 cup pasta, cooked

Salt and pepper to taste

2 teaspoons fresh parsley or tarragon, chopped

Directions:

Over medium heat, sauté the vegetables in the oil in a stockpot until the onions are transparent.

Add the Chicken Stock. Bring to a boil and then reduce to a simmer.

When the vegetables are cooked, add the chicken and pasta and return to a boil.

Season with salt and pepper and parsley or tarragon and serve.

Country Vegetable Soup

Serves 10

To get the most flavor from this hearty soup, add in a hard cheese rind (wrapped and tied tightly in a cheesecloth) just after adding the stock, and let it sit for the duration of the cooking.

Ingredients:

½ tablespoon roasted garlic paste

½ cup white onions, diced

1 summer squash, cut into half-moon slices

1 zucchini, cut into half-moon slices

1 carrot, cut into half-moon slices

1 stalk of celery, sliced into pieces on the bias

½ of 1 bulb of fennel, cut into small strips

4 tablespoons extra virgin olive oil

½ cup white beans, cooked

1 8-ounce can of whole tomatoes, crushed and drained well

2 quarts Chicken Stock (see page 163)

1 cup spinach

1 cup arugula

Salt and pepper

Directions:

Sauté all the vegetables except the beans, tomatoes, spinach, and arugula with the garlic paste in the olive oil until very soft.

Add the beans, tomatoes, and Chicken Stock. Cook until the beans are very soft. Stir in the arugula and spinach and season with salt and pepper.

Roasted Pumpkin Soup

Serves 4

Ingredients:

1 cup fresh pumpkin or heirloom pumpkin, cooked

½ cup white onion, julienned

2 tablespoons butter

1 quart water

1 teaspoon salt

1 teaspoon brown sugar

1 teaspoon maple syrup

1 dash cinnamon

1 dash cayenne

½ cup heavy cream

Directions:

Preheat oven to 350 degrees.

Split the pumpkins in half and de-seed. Place the pumpkins on a rack on a sheet pan and roast skin-side up for 45 to 60 minutes, until pumpkin is soft.

Remove the skins and discard. Roughly chop the pumpkin to create 1 cup.

Sauté the onion in the butter until transparent. Add the remaining ingredients and the pumpkin and cook for 1 hour on a low simmer.

Remove from the heat and puree until smooth. Serve.

Smoked Scallop Chowder

Serves 4

The recipe is full of flavor, thanks in large part to the addition of dulse, a seaweed product eaten as a snack in many areas of northern Europe. You can find it in most health food stores.

Ingredients:

For the wheat berry dulse sticks:

½ cup wheat berries

½ cup spring onion, with greens cut off and reserved for garnish

1⅓ cups high-gluten flour

5 tablespoons olive oil

¼ cup water

2 tablespoons dulse

2 tablespoons kosher salt

For the chowder:

4 pieces of live scallops (optional), in the shell, washed and cleaned

4 ounces bacon

¼ cup onion, diced

1½ cups white wine

1 cup Chicken Stock (see page 163)

3 cups heavy cream

2 tablespoons dulse

1 tablespoon thyme

8 ounces new potatoes, boiled

A pinch of chili powder

6 ounces Smoked Scallops, store-bought (or see page 80)

⅔ teaspoon salt

Pepper to taste

Directions:

To prepare the wheat berry dulse sticks: Preheat oven to 350 degrees.

Boil wheat berries until very soft (they may expand up to 2 cups' worth). Chop spring onion and caramelize.

Puree spring onion and ¾ cup of the cooked wheat berries. Combine flour, oil, water, and 2 tablespoons dulse. Add the wheat berry mixture to form a dough.

Chill, then roll dough paper-thin. Cut into ⅛-inch strips and roll in olive oil. Twist the sticks and place on a sheet pan. Bake until golden brown. Sprinkle with kosher salt.

To prepare the chowder: If using live scallops, steam them open in their shells and set aside.

In a pan, sauté bacon until lightly browned. Add onion and cook for 2 minutes. Deglaze with white wine and reduce by one-third. Add Chicken Stock, heavy cream, dulse, thyme, potatoes, and chili powder. Simmer to desired consistency.

Add Smoked Scallops to warm them. Season with salt and pepper. Pour soup over steamed scallops in shell. Garnish with wheat berry sticks and chopped greens from spring onion. Top with fresh cracked pepper to taste.

Nesenkeag Co-op Farm, Litchfield, New Hampshire

Name: Eero Ruuttila

What I make: Certified organic vegetables from about 35 acres of land. We do lots of braising greens, root crops—beets, carrots, and potatoes. We're a non-profit farm, and everything we don't sell to restaurants we donate to the New Hampshire Food Bank.

How I got started: Our farm's been around since the 1980s, when it became a non-profit farm. I've been here since 1987. We have a harvest crew of four or five people during the high season, and my wife helps with books and deliveries, and my son helps out with the tractor work.

How everything is made: There's no average day here. I'm in at 7 a.m., harvesting in the fields. When I have time, I walk the fields with my dog, which helps me prioritize everything for the day. We fill all the orders, and I do 90 percent of the tractor work and the sales. We have about 35 accounts, so afterward I write our newsletters to our restaurants so they can have some ideas of how to make the most of our products. Sometimes we're here nine, 10, or 11 hours.

How to buy good vegetables: Do your homework: Always ask your grower the best way to handle your vegetables once you get home. It's helpful to know that you don't put tomatoes in the fridge, or they'll get mushy. They can help you with everything from that to where to put your winter squash. At a restaurant, always ask what's local. Fresh is best. It's a flavor and taste advantage if produce is eaten within 24 hours of picking—after that, you start to lose flavor and nutritional value.

My favorite way to eat it all: I love it when my salad greens are at their peak. Good quality olive oil and balsamic vinegar—give me those and some good goat cheese and sea salt, and I'm as happy as can be.

Lobster Chowder

Serves 8

I gave my friend Rick the recipe years ago, and I got it back for this book.

Ingredients:

8 small lobsters or culls

1 bay leaf

½ teaspoon tarragon, chopped

½ cup white wine

½ cup butter

2 cups onion, diced

1 cup celery, diced

¼ cup sherry

1 quart heavy cream

2 quarts milk

¼ teaspoon thyme, chopped

2 medium-sized white potatoes, peeled and diced small

Salt and pepper

2 tablespoons parsley, chopped

Directions:

In a large pot, cover the lobsters with boiling water and cook for 15 minutes. Strain, reserving and setting aside the liquid. Chill the lobsters.

De-shell the lobsters and reserve the meat.

Crush the lobster bodies and shells and simmer with the reserved lobster stock, bay leaf, tarragon, and white wine for 30 minutes. Strain and set aside liquid.

Melt the butter in a large pot and sauté the onion and celery until transparent. Add the sherry and reduce by half.

Add the cream, milk, lobster, thyme, potatoes, and reserved liquid and bring to a simmer. Cook until the potatoes are just soft.

Season with salt and pepper and parsley and serve.

Ham Hock and Heirloom Bean Soup

Serves 8

This is a richly flavored soup that I recommend spicing up with the addition of chili pepper—the spice brings out the ham's smoky flavor that much more. But, of course, the spice-intolerant among us can easily omit it.

Ingredients:

1 cup dried heirloom beans

1 teaspoon hot chili pepper, minced (optional)

1 cup carrot, diced

1 cup celery, diced

1 cup onion, diced

2 tablespoons olive oil

1 cup tomato, peeled, seeded, drained, and diced

½ gallon Ham Hock Stock (see page 164)

1 cup ham hock meat, shredded or chopped

2 cups collard greens or wilting greens, julienned

Salt and pepper to taste

Directions:

Cover the beans by 2 times in water and soak overnight.

Drain the beans and put in a pot of water and cook until three-quarters of the way done. Drain and cool.

In a large pot, sauté the chili, carrot, celery, and onion in olive oil over medium-high heat until tender.

Add the tomatoes and sauté for 5 minutes, stirring to prevent burning.

Pour the stock over the vegetables, add the meat and beans, and simmer until the beans are tender.

Add the greens and cook for 10 minutes.

Season with salt and pepper and serve.

Native Onion Soup

Serves 6

Ingredients:

6 medium-sized native onions or
6 cups, julienned

4 tablespoons extra virgin olive oil

2 bay leaves

2 teaspoons fresh thyme, chopped

½ gallon Chicken Stock (see page 163)

¼ cup sherry

Salt and pepper to taste

Directions:

Peel the onions, cut in half and julienne.

Sauté the onions in the oil over medium-high heat in a large pot with the bay leaves and thyme, stirring to prevent burning.

Cook the onions until well-browned.

Add the stock and reduce the heat to a simmer. Cook for 1 hour.

Add the sherry and cook 15 minutes longer. Season with salt and pepper.

Iceberg Lettuce with Creamy Massachusetts Blue Cheese Dressing

Serves 4

Sometimes the simplest salads are the best.

Ingredients:

1 head iceberg lettuce

2 medium-sized tomatoes

½ cucumber

1 cup Creamy Blue Cheese Dressing (see page 176)

Freshly cracked pepper

Directions:

Cut the lettuce into quarters. Wash, drain, and chill.

Cut the tomatoes into quarters.

Score the sides of the cucumber and slice on the bias into 12 slices.

Arrange the vegetables on 4 plates, and serve with dressing and fresh pepper.

Westfield Farm, Hubbardston, Massachusetts

Name: Bob Stetson

What I make: Goat and cow's milk cheeses.

How I got started: It was back in 1996, and the operation was already under way. But I wanted the chance to get out of the city and to start to make something, so I bought it. These days we've got four full-time people, including my wife and me. We sell a couple thousand pounds of goat cheese a week.

How everything is made: We buy milk from local goat dairies, and we concentrate on making the cheese. We make an awful lot of plain, fresh goat cheese that consistently wins awards. We don't spend a lot of time on trucking, and we don't use any preservatives to enhance the yield. I find that other people have made those improvements in an effort to extend the cheese's shelf life. But if

you really want to keep the flavor, it's really easy to make goat cheese that tastes great, without adding all of that.

What's special about what we do: We have some unique cheeses that no one has been able to imitate. We're also very proud of our surface-ripened blue cheeses. It's just a matter of good ingredients and good controls.

How to choose a good goat cheese: Stay away from anything with a preservative—they just aren't necessary. For some blues, gently squeeze them—they should have a little bit of give. Serve them at room temperature to make the most of the flavors and texture.

My favorite way to eat it all: I love our fresh goat cheese with sundried tomatoes, chopped basil, and olive oil drizzled over it.

Roasted Beet Salad with Chèvre, Arugula, and Blood Orange Vinaigrette

Serves 6

Ingredients:

For the maple walnuts:

2 tablespoons butter

½ teaspoon salt

4 tablespoons maple syrup

1 teaspoon water

½ pound walnuts

For the salad:

12 cups arugula

1 medium-sized beet

1 tablespoon olive oil

1 tablespoon salt

Blood Orange Vinaigrette (see page 178)

12 ounces local goat cheese

¼ cup maple walnuts

Freshly cracked pepper

Directions:

To make the maple walnuts:

Preheat oven to 300 degrees.

Combine all ingredients except walnuts in a saucepan and simmer very slowly for 3 minutes.

Pour the glaze over the nuts and bake, stirring every 10 minutes, until nuts look dry (about 30 to 40 minutes).

To make the salad:

Preheat oven to 350 degrees.

Wash the arugula, spin it dry, and set aside.

Rub the beet lightly with oil, sprinkle with salt, and bake in the oven until cooked through, approximately 45 minutes.

Cool the beet enough to handle, and then peel by rubbing it in your hands with a kitchen towel. Cool the beet to room temperature.

Toss the arugula in three-quarters of the dressing.

Arrange the arugula on a plate, and thinly shave the beet over the greens using a potato peeler.

Crumble the cheese over the salad, drizzle with the remaining dressing, sprinkle with the nuts and top with fresh cracked pepper.

Spinach Salad with Goat Cheese and Spicy Pecans

Serves 6

*This is our best-selling salad at Henrietta's Table;
it comes from my old sous chef Todd Young.*

Ingredients:

For the spicy pecans:

2⅛ ounces pecan halves, toasted

2 teaspoons cumin

¼ teaspoon chili powder

¼ teaspoon cayenne pepper

1 teaspoon thyme

¼ teaspoon cardamom

¼ teaspoon cinnamon

2 teaspoons paprika

¼ teaspoon salt

½ ounce butter

2 teaspoons maple syrup

For the salad:

12 ounces fresh spinach

2 cups Maple-Pecan Vinaigrette
(see page 177)

2 ounces goat cheese

½ pint fresh berries

Directions:

To make the spicy pecans:

Toast pecans until golden brown.

Mix dry ingredients together in a medium-sized bowl.

Melt the butter in a pan and add maple syrup, bring to a boil and remove from heat. Pour butter mixture over pecans and toss.

Sprinkle entire spice mixture over pecans and toss until well coated. Set aside to dry for 1 hour or up to 2 days.

To make the salad:

Wash the spinach and dry in a salad spinner.

Toss with the dressing and the spicy pecans, goat cheese, and berries.

Serve immediately.

Romaine Salad with Creamy Garlic Dressing

Serves 6

Ingredients:

1½ heads romaine lettuce

1 loaf French bread, diced

¼ cup extra virgin olive oil

2 tablespoons mixed herbs, chopped

1 cup Creamy Garlic Dressing
(see page 172)

¼ cup Parmesan, grated

1 roasted red pepper, seeded, peeled, and diced

Freshly cracked black pepper

Directions:

Preheat oven to 350 degrees.

Cut the romaine into quarters lengthwise. Wash and drain thoroughly. Set aside and chill.

Toss the bread with the oil and herbs and toast in the oven until crisp (about 20 minutes). Set aside to cool at room temperature.

Arrange the romaine on a plate, top with the dressing, cheese, croutons, and roasted red pepper.

Top with fresh black pepper to taste and serve.

Farmer's Cheese Salad

Serves 6

Ingredients:

3 quarts water

½ pound cheese curd

2 cups buttermilk

6 ounces kosher salt

4 cups ice

4 tablespoons extra virgin olive oil

½ cup fresh basil

Directions:

In a saucepan, heat water to 160 degrees.

Crumble cheese curd into ¾-inch chunks.

Add the buttermilk to the curd, and add the salt. Let mixture stand for 15 to 20 minutes.

Add 1 quart of the 160-degree water to the curd mix. Mix with hands to stir salt through the curd. Drain into colander, and return the curd back into the bowl.

Add 160-degree water to cover curd and let sit for 3 to 5 minutes, adding small amounts of 160-degree water to the bowl to keep the curd temperature at 160 degrees.

Work cheese until pliable and form into balls, being careful not to overwork it; the cheese should have an elastic and melting consistency.

Stretch and drip cheese into small balls, then place in ice bath. Chill for 20 to 30 minutes, or until cheese is set. Wrap cheese in plastic wrap tightly.

To make the dressing:
Mix the olive oil and basil in a blender until mixed thoroughly. Serve cheese with the dressing.

Shy Brothers' Hannahbells cheese

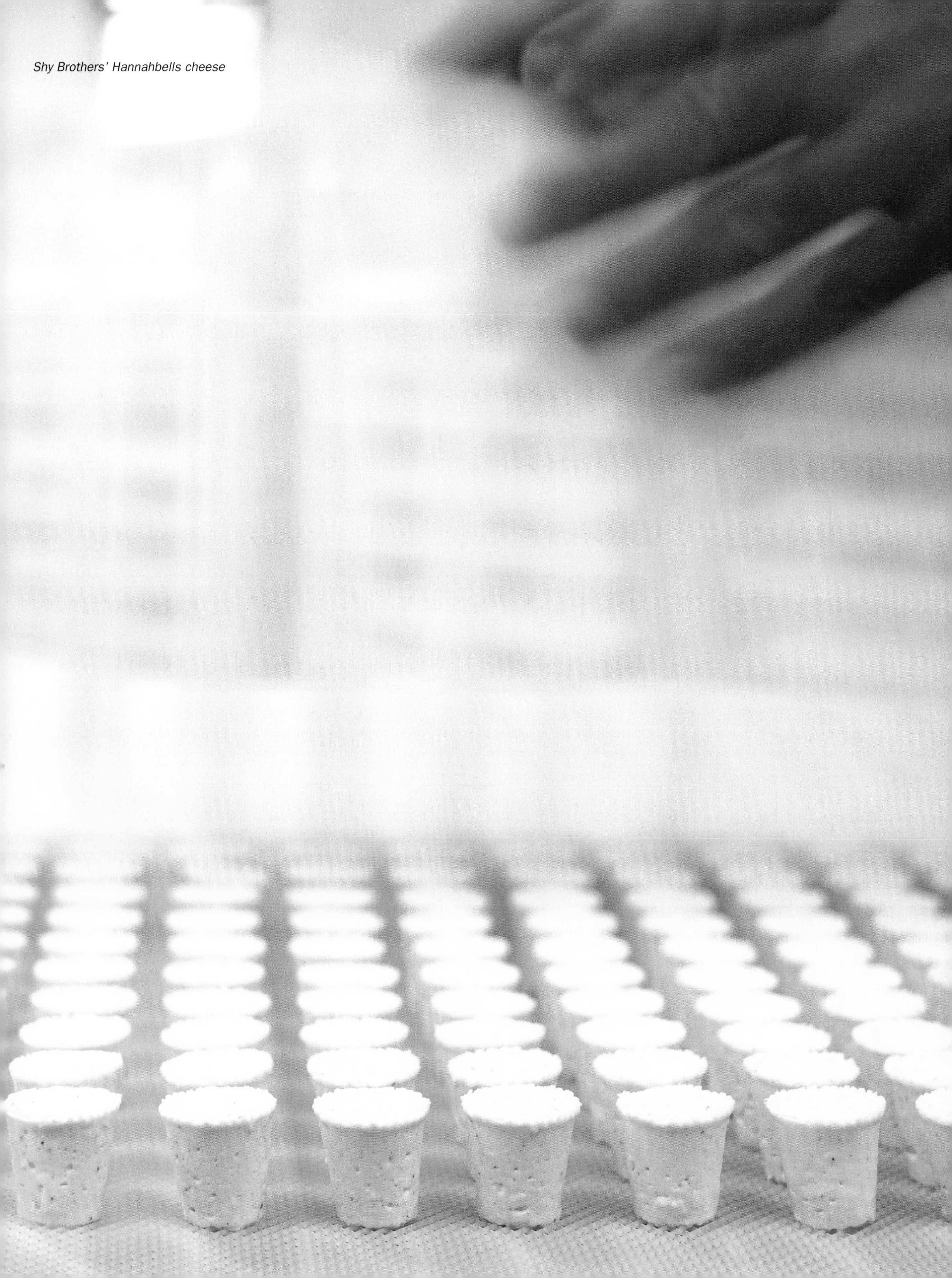

Starters

Tapenade
Bread

In my mind, how you begin a meal is as important as the entirety of what follows. Starters set the tone, get your appetite really going, and rev up your taste buds for the courses ahead. So with that in mind, they should stay within the character of the rest of the meal. Just as I don't like to serve overly wrought entrees, I also don't like to serve fussy, overly constructed introductions; my favorite appetizers highlight a few well-balanced tastes and textures—all of them as fresh as possible—and then back off, leaving diners a little less hungry, but with plenty of room for all that comes next.

Spiced Olives

Serves 8 to 10

Ingredients:

8 ounce can black olives, drained

8 ounce jar green olives, drained

2 tablespoons flat-leaf parsley, roughly chopped

2 tablespoons cilantro, roughly chopped

½ cup lemon juice

½ cup extra virgin olive oil

2 tablespoons cumin seed

1 tablespoon red pepper flakes

Zest of 1 medium orange, chopped

Zest of 1 medium lemon, chopped

Zest of 1 medium lime, chopped

Salt and pepper to taste

Directions:

In a large bowl, toss all ingredients together until combined well.

Season to taste. Let sit for 3 to 4 days before serving.

Tapenade Bread

Serves 4

Ingredients:

¼ cup sundried tomatoes

¼ cup pitted Kalamata olives

¼ cup pitted Sicilian green olives

1 cup capers

¼ cup olive oil

Salt and pepper

1 loaf French bread

Directions:

Place all ingredients except the bread in a food processor and pulse until it becomes a coarse spread.

Slice the bread in half lengthwise. Sprinkle with a little olive oil, salt, and pepper.

Grill or toast bread crust-side up until lightly browned. Remove from heat, and spread the olive mixture over the bread. Cut in 2 inch–long pieces and serve.

Bluefish Pâté

Serves 8

Ingredients:

1½ pounds smoked bluefish

5 ounces cream cheese

1 cup heavy cream

4 tablespoons red onion, minced

2 tablespoons chives, finely chopped

2 tablespoons chervil, chopped

4 tablespoons fresh lemon juice

Salt and pepper to taste

Directions:

Cut the bluefish into small pieces and chill.

Place the chilled bluefish into a food processor and puree, adding in the cream cheese slowly. Blend until smooth. Slowly add the heavy cream until incorporated into the mix.

Remove from the food processor and fold in the onion, herbs, lemon juice, salt and pepper. Serve or chill until ready to serve.

New England Cheese Board

Serves 6

Ingredients:

(As shown from bottom to top):

Hubbardston blue goat cheese,
Westfield Farm, Massachusetts

Ben Nevis,
Bonnieview Farm, Vermont

Bayley Hazen Blue,
Jasper Hill Farm, Vermont

Cambridge Reserve,
West River Creamery, Vermont

Hannahbells,
Shy Brothers Farm, Massachusetts

Directions:

Arrange local cheeses on a nice
cutting board.

Serve with dried apricots, fresh fruit,
Spicy Pecans (see page 60), local
honey, preserves, and other crackers and
condiments of your choice.

Crab Cakes

Serves 6

To me, these cakes are the essence of New England. I suggest serving them on vegetable slaw or with grilled asparagus and Tartar Sauce.

Ingredients:

¼ loaf white bread slices, crust removed

2 pounds fresh rock crabmeat

3½ tablespoons Dijon mustard

¾ cup mayonnaise

1 dash Old Bay Seasoning

¼ cup asparagus, steamed and diced

2 tablespoons butter

Tartar Sauce (see page 160)

Directions:

Cut bread in small dice.

Mix all ingredients except butter in a large bowl until well blended. Use 2 hands to mold individually-sized cakes from the mixture.

In a medium-sized saucepan, heat butter until just melted, and sauté the cakes. Serve immediately with Tartar Sauce.

Duck Pastrami

Serves 4

Ingredients:

2 duck breasts

1 cup Wet Brine (see page 165)

¼ cup Pastrami Rub (see page 166)

¼ cup hardwood chips

Directions:

Soak the breasts in the brine for 12 hours.

Remove the breasts and coat with the Pastrami Rub.

Soak the wood chips in water for 5 minutes. Wrap loosely in foil. Place the wood chips on the fire in a covered gas grill.

When the chips begin to smoke heavily, extinguish the fire and place the duck breasts on a rack over a shallow pan of ice. Place into the grill and cover immediately.

Let the duck smoke for 1 hour.

Preheat oven to 350 degrees.

Remove the duck from the grill and place in the oven. Cook to an internal temperature of 125 degrees.

Remove from the oven and chill in the refrigerator.

When ready to serve, slice thinly.

Grit Cakes with Mushrooms

Serves 4

*If you can't find good, fresh stone-ground grits,
substitute stone-ground polenta instead.*

Ingredients:

2½ cups water

1 cup coarse grits

4 tablespoons chives, chopped

¼ cup goat cheese

Salt and pepper

½ cup button mushrooms,
cut into quarters

¼ cup shiitake mushrooms, sliced

½ cup portobello mushrooms, sliced

¼ cup oyster mushrooms, sliced

4 tablespoons olive oil

½ cup flageolet beans, cooked

4 Roma tomatoes, cut into quarters and
oven-dried

1 teaspoon thyme, chopped

¼ cup sherry

¼ cup butter

Directions:

In a saucepan, bring the water to a boil. Stir in the grits and cook until tender. Remove from the stove, stir in the chives and cheese. Season with salt and pepper.

Spread the grits mixture across a flat pan evenly, to about a ½-inch thickness. Let cool.

Sauté all of the mushrooms in olive oil until tender. Add the beans, tomatoes, and thyme and heat through. Add the sherry and reduce by half. Cut the butter into slices and add to the mixture until melted, just keeping the mixture warm—do not boil the butter.

Cut the grits into 4 cakes and sear on both sides. Arrange on a serving plate, and pour the mushroom mixture over them.

Cod Fish Cakes

Serves 6

Ingredients:

1 pound salt cod

2 pounds white potatoes, peeled and halved

½ of 1 onion, chopped

4 tablespoons butter

1 dash Worcestershire sauce

1 egg

3 egg yolks

1¾ teaspoons fresh thyme, chopped

1¾ teaspoons chives, chopped

3 dashes olive oil

Directions:

Soak the cod in cold water for 24 hours. Remove from the water and boil in new water for 5 minutes. Drain and break into flakes and keep warm.

Boil potatoes in salted water until knife-tender. Drain and make sure potatoes are dry, then mash by hand.

Cook the onion in butter until transparent. In a large bowl, mix the onion, potatoes, and cod together with the rest of the ingredients. Cool.

Use 2 hands to mold the mixture into individually-sized cakes.

Just before serving, in a medium-sized saucepan, heat olive oil until just sizzling, and sauté the cakes. Serve immediately.

Eva's Garden, South Dartmouth, Massachusetts

Name: Eva Sommaripa

What I make: Organic culinary herbs, baby greens, and flowers. I grow many varieties of each— from bronze fennel and chervil to chickweed and cress.

How I got started: I've been supplying Boston-area restaurants for more than 30 years. But I originally trained as a potter at the Rhode Island School of Design, and worked as an artist in Cambridge. I had a garden in Dartmouth then, and was growing things for myself. Before I knew it, I was selling herbs to grocery stores, restaurants, and then I just expanded from there.

How everything gets made: I pick everything so it's incredibly fresh. This optimizes flavor and shelf life. And I only pick to order.

How to use it in the kitchen: Use the greens as simply as possible. Remember, the more flavors you put on them, the more you'll miss the greens, which have such different and wonderful flavors and textures of their own, and they can get lost in a flavorful dressing.

My favorite way to eat it all: Either eat a naked salad or add a splash of good olive oil and salt at the last moment.

Massachusetts Oysters, Preserved Lemon Maine Vodka and Horseradish

Serves 6

For this dish I prefer oysters from Duxbury Bay or Wellfleet, Massachusetts—they're incredibly plump and briny, and have a subtle butteriness to them. But of course, use whatever your best local oyster is, and odds are you won't go wrong.

Ingredients:

6 ounces Cold River Vodka

6 tablespoons Preserved Lemons, finely diced (see page 158)

2 dozen oysters

4 tablespoons shallots, minced

4 teaspoons horseradish

Directions:

Mix the vodka and the Preserved Lemons and set aside.

Open the oysters and keep well chilled.

Add the shallots to the vodka and spoon evenly on top of the oysters.

Top each oyster with the horseradish and serve immediately.

Grilled Native Asparagus, Feta, and EVOO

Serves 6

If you can get your hands on Vermont-made feta for this dish, I highly recommend it. It has a creamier-than-usual quality that brings out the sweetness of the asparagus.

Ingredients:

2 tablespoons Preserved Lemons (see page 158), finely diced

¼ cup extra virgin olive oil

1½ pounds native asparagus

2 cups arugula

12 ounces feta

Freshly cracked pepper

Directions:

Marinate the Preserved Lemons in the olive oil and let it sit overnight.

Peel the stems of the asparagus and poach the stalks until just tender in well-salted water. Remove and place immediately in ice water.

Wash and dry the arugula and arrange on a plate with the asparagus and feta. Drizzle with the oil and top with pepper to taste.

Smoked Scallops

Serves 4

Ingredients:

For the brine:

1 cup salt

⅓ cup white pepper

⅙ cup sugar

1 teaspoon fresh thyme, chopped

For the scallops:

6 ounces bay scallops

1 ounce apple wood chips

Directions:

To prepare the brine:

Mix all of the brine ingredients together.

To prepare the scallops:

Place half of the brine on a tray and layer the scallops on top of it. Pour the remaining brine over the scallops and let sit for 2 hours. Rinse the brine off and let dry overnight.

In a smoker, heat the wood chips until they begin to smoke. Place a pan of ice over the chips, and on top of that, set a rack. Set the scallops on the rack (do not let the scallops touch the ice). Cover the smoker to retain the smoke. Extinguish any heat in the smoker so the chips cease smoking, and let sit 45 minutes.

Remove the scallops from the smoker and keep refrigerated until ready to serve.

Great Hill Blue Farm
Marion, Massachusetts

Name: Tim Stone

What I make: Cow's milk blue cheese.

How I got started: After selling milk, I wanted to stay in the dairy business and decided to focus on blue cheese after researching and discovering that none was being made in the East with cow's milk.

How I make everything: Almost everything is created by hand—except our wheel punches, which are done with a pneumatic machine.

What's special about what we do: We're the only ones making this kind of cheese with non-homogenized milk. That requires more aging (and therefore more time), but it results in a smooth, non-acidic finish.

How to use it in the kitchen: It's terrific in salads, on crackers, and it melts incredibly well on top of meat and burgers.

My favorite way to eat it all: The simplest way possible—meaning on a bland cracker with wine, or beer (my personal favorite).

Homemade Smoked Salmon

Serves 6

Ingredients:

3 cups Dry Brine (see page 165)

12 ounces salmon filet, skin on

¼ cup apple wood chips
(or any hardwood chip)

3 cups field greens

3 tablespoons grapeseed oil

12 bagel chips

1 lemon, cut into 6 wedges

Directions:

Pour one-quarter of the brine into a casserole dish and place the salmon skin-side down on top of it. Pour the remaining brine over the salmon and refrigerate for 8 hours.

Remove the salmon from the refrigerator and wash the brine off with cold water. Place on a rack and put back in the refrigerator, uncovered, for 12 hours.

Soak the wood chips in water for 5 minutes. Wrap in foil loosely.

Place the wood chips on the fire of a covered gas (not charcoal) grill.

When the wood chips begin to smoke heavily, extinguish the fire and place the salmon (still on the rack and tray) onto a pan of ice and into the smoker. Place the cover on the grill.

Let the salmon smoke for 30 minutes. Then remove from the grill and refrigerate overnight.

Remove the skin from the salmon with a sharp knife.

Slice the salmon as thinly as possible. Divide and arrange the greens onto plates. Divide and set the salmon on top. Drizzle with the oil and serve with the bagel chips and lemon wedges.

Grilled Portobello with Vermont Blythedale Farm Brie and Walnut Vinaigrette

Serves 4

*If you can't find Vermont Blythedale Farm Brie nearby,
use your favorite locally made, creamy, mild cheese.*

Ingredients:

4 medium-sized portobello caps

1 batch Mushroom Marinade
(see page 170)

Salt and pepper

2 ounces Vermont Brie

6 ounces mesclun mix

1 batch Walnut Vinaigrette
(see page 174)

Directions:

Brine the mushrooms for 2 hours in the marinade. Drain the mushrooms well, and season with salt and pepper.

Preheat oven to 350 degrees.

Grill mushrooms over medium heat, turning regularly to prevent burning. When the mushrooms are cooked through, remove from the grill and cool.

Place a slice of Brie on each of the mushroom caps and place in the oven for 5 minutes.

Divide the mesclun on 4 plates. Put a mushroom on each plate and top with the Walnut Vinaigrette.

The dining room at Henrietta's Table

Lunch & Dinner

Pot Roast

As a lover of both food and countryside, I've always counted myself truly lucky to live in New England—the junction of incredible farmland (meaning turf-based delicacies like poultry and meats) and oceans and bays galore (which yield world-envied lobsters, oysters, scallops, clams, and fish of every permutation and of the ultimate freshness). These are the things that make living here a blessing, and they're also the things that make mealtime something to really, really look forward to. Caught in season, bluefish arrives in the kitchens of Henrietta's Table as rich and briny as anything I've ever tasted, and all it requires is some added smokiness and acidic lightness to bring its deep flavor to a crescendo. In fall, nothing can compare to the sweet earthiness of wild duck or the spicy complexity of venison cooked just right. And all year long, the people at farms like River Rock in Brimfield, Massachusetts, lovingly tend grass-fed, conscientiously-raised herds that yield some of the most velvety cuts of beef out there. These are the flavors that well deserve their place as the spotlight of a meal, and as something to look forward to all day—if not all year—long.

Seafood

Cornmeal-Crusted Monkfish Sandwich

Serves 4

Ingredients:

1 pound monkfish

½ cup flour

1 cup fine cornmeal

1 teaspoon Old Bay Seasoning

1 cup buttermilk

¼ cup butter, melted

2 tablespoons Thai chili garlic sauce

4 tablespoons Tartar Sauce (see page 160)

4 bulky rolls

1 tomato, sliced

4 large lettuce leaves

Directions:

Slice the fish on the diagonal, into ¼-inch thick pieces.

Mix the flour, cornmeal, and Old Bay Seasoning together. Dip the filets into the buttermilk and then the cornmeal mix, patting to coat the fish evenly.

In a skillet over medium heat, cook the fish in the butter, lightly browning on both sides.

Mix the Thai chili garlic sauce into the Tartar Sauce to give it some spice.

Spread each roll evenly with the spicy Tartar Sauce and arrange the fish, tomato, and lettuce on the rolls. Serve immediately.

Grilled Citrus- and Dill-Cured Sablefish

Serves 6

The marinade for this dish also works well with salmon.

Ingredients:

½ cup dill

1 teaspoon juniper berry

1 tablespoon coriander seed

½ of 1 carrot

½ of 1 leek

½ cup salt

½ cup sugar

1 cup fresh orange juice

1 cup fresh lemon juice

6 4-ounce sable filets, skinned

12 ounces fresh asparagus

6 ounces crème fraîche

Directions:

In a food processor, grind the dill, juniper, coriander, carrot, and leek. Combine the ground ingredients with the salt, sugar, and juices. Pour the mixture over the fish filets and marinate for 4 hours, then rinse the marinade off of the fish.

Poach the asparagus in salted water and plunge into a bowl of cold water to immediately cool.

Grill the fish until cooked through.

Arrange the fish over the asparagus and drizzle with the crème fraîche to serve.

New England Lobster Bake

Ingredients:

8 medium-sized red-skinned potatoes

4 1½-pound live lobsters

4 ears fresh corn, unhusked

2 pounds steamer clams

4 pieces of cheesecloth, cut into 18-inch squares

1 pound seaweed

1 pound butter

2 lemons, halved

Directions:

Preheat oven to 350 degrees.

Boil the potatoes for 5 minutes, then cool.

On each piece of cheesecloth, place 1 lobster, 1 ear of corn, ½ pound of steamers, and 2 potatoes. Fold up the edges of the cheesecloth to form a sack and tie shut. Repeat with the remaining ingredients to form 4 sacks.

Place the seaweed in the bottom of a heavy-bottomed pan large enough to hold the 4 lobster sacks. Place the sack on top of the seaweed and cover the pan with aluminum foil.

Place the pan over a hot stove or char-grill for 10 minutes. Remove and put into the oven for about 15 minutes or until the lobster is cooked.

While the sacks are cooking, melt the butter over low heat.

Remove the sacks from the pan and serve with the melted butter and lemon halves.

Ted Mahoney, Nahant, Massachusetts

Name: Ted Mahoney

What I do: I'm a commercial lobsterman.

How I got started: I've been doing this for a long time. I started when I was a young kid; I had a skiff and just did it for fun. Then for years after that I taught school and fished part-time, and then finally went full-time as a fisherman in 1980. I've been doing it as a full-time job ever since.

My typical day: I typically get up around 4 a.m., and meet my stern man by 5. We're usually hauling the first trawl between 5 and 6 a.m. I haul 15 to 17 trawls a day, which means we do just under 300 traps a day. By 1 or 2 in the afternoon, we're done on the boat and bringing the lobsters right to the fish market. Then we start making arrangements for the next day, deal with any maintenance on the boat, and any other problems that need fixing.

How I harvest: With prices for fuel and bait higher than usual, you have to catch over 100 pounds of lobster a day to make any profit. I fish from the first of May until just before Christmas. Some guys fish all year long, but that is really hard on you and your equipment.

How to pick them: Of course you want to buy them live, and go to a place that has a quick turnover, so you know they're fresh. Lots of supermarkets have lobsters that have been in the tanks for days, or sometimes they come from a pound, which means the flavor won't be as good.

My favorite way to eat it all: My wife is a fantastic cook, and I love to eat lobster lots of different ways. But if you get the right ones, you don't need anything but lemon and butter. My favorites are the soft shell—not the new shell, but soft shell. You don't get as much meat, but it's better and much, much sweeter.

Finnan Haddie

Serves 6

Ingredients:

8 medium-sized red potatoes

2 pounds smoked haddock

1 medium-sized white onion

2 cups heavy cream

1 cup light cream

¼ teaspoon Old Bay Seasoning

½ teaspoon thyme, chopped

1½ pounds asparagus

Directions:

Blanch and slice the potatoes to ½-inch thick. Set aside.

Cut the fish into 6 equal portions.

Slice the onion into ⅛-inch rings.

Place the onions and cream in a saucepan and set on low heat. Once simmering, add the fish to poach. Sprinkle with Old Bay Seasoning, and thyme.

In a separate bowl, blanch the asparagus in salted water and chill immediately.

When the onions are tender and the fish is heated through (approximately 20 minutes), add in the potato and cook for 5 more minutes.

Reheat the asparagus and place on top of the fish.

Serve immediately.

Poached Salmon Roll

Serves 6

Ingredients:

1 lemon, halved

1 tablespoon peppercorns

4 tablespoons flat-leaf parsley, coarsely chopped, stems removed

1 2½-pound skinless salmon fillet

Salt and pepper to taste

4 tablespoons tarragon, coarsely chopped, stems removed

Directions:

Fill an 8-inch-deep pan halfway with water, add the lemon, peppercorns, and parsley and heat to a simmer.

Butterfly salmon from middle outward, in both directions.

Season with salt and pepper.

Sprinkle the chopped tarragon on opened filets.

Roll salmon up tightly by hand like a jelly roll, and wrap in plastic wrap. Tie ends together.

Poach salmon in seasoned water until it reaches 160 degrees.

Remove salmon from poaching liquid and let cool. Remove plastic wrap, slice and serve on a platter alongside lemon.

Mussels Dijon

Serves 4

Here's a New England version of the old French classic, sparked up by plenty of garlic. It's great served over a few slices of grilled baguette, which soak up the sauce nicely.

Ingredients:

2 tablespoons shallots, chopped

1 tablespoon garlic, chopped

4 tablespoons olive oil

3 pounds mussels, rinsed and debearded

½ cup dry white wine

4 tablespoons Dijon mustard

1 cup heavy cream

1 tablespoon chives, sliced thinly

Directions:

Sauté the shallots and garlic in the olive oil. Add the mussels, wine, mustard, and cream.

Simmer the mussels until they open. Remove from the heat and pour into shallow soup bowls.

Garnish with chives and serve immediately.

Salmon Burgers

Serves 4

Ingredients:

1½ pounds salmon filet

4 tablespoons panko bread crumbs

2 tablespoons fresh chives, chopped

4 tablespoons Dijon mustard

Salt and pepper

4 bulky rolls

4 leaves of red leaf lettuce

1 tomato, sliced

Tartar Sauce (see page 160)

Directions:

Chop the salmon into a fine dice by hand.

Mix the salmon with the bread crumbs, chives, and mustard in a bowl over ice to keep the fish mixture well chilled.

Portion the mix into 4 burgers.

Season with salt and pepper and grill for approximately 10 minutes on each side over medium heat.

Serve on the bulky rolls with lettuce, tomato, and Tartar Sauce.

Woodbury's Seafood, Wellfleet, Massachusetts

Name: Pat Woodbury

What I do: I harvest clams and oysters.

How I got started: We've been doing this for 22 years. My wife and I were grad students in marine biology together, and we knew some folks doing aquaculture on Cape Cod, and decided to join them instead of staying in academia. We did it and never left.

How I harvest: We're on a lunar schedule, because we work at low tide on the flats. That changes every day by an hour, so it's always a little different. We harvest twice a week for restaurant customers, and then go back in our shop to sort and grade according to size. After that, I'll start calling our restaurants for deliveries.

What's special about what we do: Shellfish are far better just after harvesting, and with us, everything gets packed to order, and then we leave the next morning to distribute everything.

How to pick them: First, go to a fish market that you trust. You can tell a lot about shellfish by using all of your senses. Ask when it was harvested—most clams and oysters have a shelf life of about a week. Try to smell it—it should be fresh—and everything should be

tightly closed. When they warm up a little, they'll open up. If you tap the shell, they should close up tightly.

My favorite way to eat it all: I love to pop a littleneck on the grill rack for a minute. Add olive oil, pepper, and garlic. I also love them nice and cold on the half-shell. Maybe add just a little touch of lemon and a tiny bit of horseradish. The essence is the briny, sweet flavor of the ocean.

Hot Smoked Bluefish with Beach Plum Vinaigrette

Serves 4

This smoky rendition of bluefish and sweet-tart dressing is perfect when served with either crisp salad greens or mashed potatoes. This recipe is for the oven, but can also be made outside on your grill.

Ingredients:

10 ounces beach plum jelly

¼ cup water

3 tablespoons Champagne vinegar

2 ounces wood chips

4 8-ounce bluefish filets

Directions:

Preheat oven to 350 degrees.

To make the vinaigrette:

Over medium heat, combine jelly, water, and vinegar in a saucepan until it becomes liquid. Set aside to cool.

To make the fish:

In an ovenproof baking pan, place a layer of foil, covered by a layer of wood chips. Place a rack over the wood chip layer, set the bluefish on the rack, and cover the pan with aluminum foil.

Cook on the stovetop over high heat until the wood chips begin to smoke. Remove from heat and place in the oven for 20 minutes.

Drizzle the bluefish with beach plum vinaigrette and serve with either greens or mashed potatoes.

Maple Thyme~Glazed Salmon

Serves 4

Ingredients:

2 tablespoons maple sugar

1 tablespoon fresh thyme leaves

1 tablespoon maple syrup

¼ cup Pommerey mustard

2 tablespoons horseradish

3 tablespoons maple syrup

½ cup water

4 8-ounce salmon filets

Directions:

Preheat oven to 325 degrees.

Mix sugar, thyme, and 1 tablespoon maple syrup to make a glaze.

Mix all the remaining ingredients except the salmon in a bowl to make the vinaigrette.

Coat the salmon with the maple glaze and place it in the oven for 12 to 15 minutes. Remove and serve with the vinaigrette.

Scrod

Serves 6

This is my mother's and grandmother's recipe, and I haven't found one better.

Ingredients:

1½ cups Ritz Crackers, lightly crushed

2 tablespoons fresh parsley, chopped

6 8-ounce pieces scrod

Salt and pepper to taste

½ cup butter, clarified

1½ lemons, cut into quarters

Directions:

Preheat oven to 350 degrees.

In a bowl, combine the crushed crackers with the parsley.

Season the fish with salt and pepper and dredge in the butter.

Place the fish on a baking tray, and sprinkle heavily with the cracker mix. Bake in the oven for 10 to 15 minutes or until the fish is cooked through.

Serve with fresh lemon.

Pizza of Maine Rock Crab, Dulse, and Sea Salt

Serves 8

Ingredients:

For the pizza dough (makes enough for 8 individual pizzas):

1¼ cups water

½ tablespoon fresh yeast

⅜ cup olive oil

2½ cups all-purpose flour

¾ cup bread flour

1½ tablespoons sugar

1½ tablespoons salt

For the pizza:

2 vine-ripened red tomatoes, cored

2 vine-ripened yellow tomatoes, cored

½ cup crème fraîche

2 pounds fresh Maine crab leg meat

Sea salt

4 tablespoons dulse seaweed, chopped

4 ounces arugula

¼ cup extra virgin olive oil

Directions:

For the pizza dough:

In a bowl with dough hook, add water and yeast, mix to dissolve.

Add olive oil and flours, followed by sugar and salt. Mix with dough hook for 5 minutes. Let dough rest for approximately 30 minutes, covered.

Divide dough into 8 pieces and round into 8 balls. Let rest for 10 more minutes, covered.

Preheat oven to 375 degrees.

With a rolling pin, roll each piece into a round flat pizza shape. Brush each with olive oil.

Let the dough rest and rise for about 20 minutes.

Bake until golden brown.

For the pizza:

Slice the tomatoes into ⅛-inch slices.

When the dough is cooked, spread the top with crème fraîche.

Layer the tomatoes around in alternating colors. Sprinkle the crabmeat over the top and season with sea salt and dulse.

Garnish with arugula and drizzle with olive oil to serve.

Grilled Striped Bass with Warm Fruit Salad and Pea Tendrils

Serves 4

This dish is one of the spring specialties at Henrietta's Table; it's such a stylish and colorful way to enjoy the natural flavors of the ingredients, it's tough to believe how easy it is to prepare.

Ingredients:

½ cup fiddleheads

¼ cup ramps

¼ cup extra virgin olive oil

1 teaspoon fresh tarragon, finely chopped

3 tablespoons tequila

1 cup fresh orange juice

1 fresh peach, pitted and sliced

1 nectarine, pitted and sliced

1 plum, pitted and sliced

Salt and pepper to taste

4 8-ounce striped bass filets

1 pound pea tendrils

Directions:

To make the fiddleheads and ramps:

Blanch the fiddleheads in boiling salted water until tender, then cool quickly by submerging in ice water. Wash the ramps well to remove any dirt. Lightly spray the ramps with olive oil and grill over medium heat. Set aside to cool.

To make the fruit:

Combine the olive oil, tarragon, tequila, and orange juice in a small bowl and set aside. Season the peaches, nectarines, and plums lightly with salt and pepper, and grill over high heat until seared, but still firm. Remove the fruit from the flame and place into the orange juice mixture to let it mellow into a vinaigrette. Cover and keep warm.

For the bass:

Season the bass lightly with salt and pepper and grill over high heat until tender—fish will flake when pierced with a fork. Remove and keep warm.

To assemble everything:

Sauté the fiddleheads and ramps and mix with the pea tendrils. Place the bass on top of the salad and top with grilled fruit. Spoon orange juice vinaigrette over the top and serve.

Meat

Pale Ale~Braised Short Ribs

Serves 4

Ingredients:

4 tablespoons canola oil

4 short ribs

Salt and pepper to taste

1 stalk celery, chopped

½ of 1 carrot, chopped

2 medium-sized onions, peeled and chopped

1 cup pale ale beer

2 bay leaves

3 cups Chicken Stock (see page 163)

1 cup Veal or Oxtail Stock (see page 164)

Directions:

Place the oil in a heavy-bottomed pot over medium heat.

Season the ribs with salt and pepper and place in the oil, browning on all sides.

Remove the ribs from the pan and add in the chopped vegetables, lightly browning. Pour the beer over the vegetables and reduce by two-thirds. Add the bay leaves, Chicken Stock, and Veal or Oxtail Stock, and place the ribs back in the pan.

Cover the pan and cook lightly, simmering until the ribs are tender, about 2 to 3 hours.

Remove the ribs from the liquid, pour out the excess grease, and reduce the liquid until it coats the back of a spoon. Strain the sauce.

When ready to serve, heat the short ribs in the sauce and transfer to a plate.

BBQ Grilled and Braised Lamb Shanks

Serves 4

*These fall-off-the-bone, delicious shanks are terrific served
with wilted greens, spinach, or braised collards.*

Ingredients:

4 lamb shanks

¼ cup Dry BBQ Rub (see page 166)

1 gallon Chicken Stock (see page 163)

½ cup Bourbon BBQ Sauce (see page 162)

Directions:

Rub the shanks with the Dry BBQ Rub until totally covered.

Place shanks on a hot grill and cook on all sides until lightly charred.

Remove the shanks and put them in a heavy-bottomed saucepot and cover with the stock.

Place on the stove and bring to a boil, then reduce to a simmer.

Cook the shanks until the meat is tender and pulls from the bone (approximately 3 hours).

Remove the shanks from the pan and reduce the sauce to desired consistency. Then add the Bourbon BBQ Sauce, and cook for 10 more minutes.

While the shanks are still warm, pull the meat from the bone.

Place the meat back in the sauce to reheat and serve.

Maple-Marinated Leg of Lamb
with Rosemary- and Garlic-Herbed Potatoes

Serves 6

Ingredients:

For the marinade:

1 cup soy sauce

2 teaspoons garlic, chopped

1 cup balsamic vinegar

1 sprig fresh thyme

1 cup maple syrup

1 cup water

For the lamb:

1 6-pound boneless leg of lamb, rolled and tied

Salt and pepper

10 purple potatoes, cut into quarters

5 Yukon Gold potatoes, cut into quarters

2 teaspoons garlic, chopped

½ pound butter, cubed

1 cup Chicken Stock
(see page 163)

3 teaspoons fresh parsley, chopped

1 teaspoon fresh rosemary, chopped

1 teaspoon fresh thyme, chopped

2 teaspoons fresh chives, chopped

Directions:

Mix all marinade ingredients thoroughly.

Marinate lamb overnight in the refrigerator, covered tightly with plastic wrap.

Preheat oven to 350 degrees.

Remove the lamb from the marinade.

Place lamb in a roasting pan and season with salt and pepper. Place the pan in the oven and cook for approximately 1 hour.

Remove and let rest for 30 minutes before carving.

Blanch the potatoes separately in boiling salted water until tender.

Sauté the chopped garlic in 1 tablespoon of butter until transparent. Add the potatoes, Chicken Stock, and chopped herbs. Cook until the potatoes are fork-tender. Coat potatoes with remaining butter.

To serve, slice lamb onto a platter and serve alongside potatoes.

Pulled Pork

Serves 10

Ingredients:

4 pounds pork butt

½ cup Dry BBQ Rub (see page 166)

2 pounds smoked ham hocks

10 Roma tomatoes, char-grilled

1 dried ancho pepper

2 ounces chipotle peppers in adobe sauce, store-bought

2 poblano peppers, grilled, peeled, and seeded

4 tablespoons molasses

Directions:

Rub the pork butt with the Dry BBQ Rub and smoke at 170 degrees for 7 hours, or until it reaches an internal temperature of 165 degrees.

Fill one-quarter of a heavy-bottomed pan with water and cook the ham hocks over medium heat for 4 hours.

Put the remaining ingredients in a pot and add the smoked butts and ham hocks and simmer over low heat for 2 to 3 hours, adding water to moisten if necessary.

Pull meat apart using a meat fork to shred it.

Ham and Potato Casserole

Serves 6

Ingredients:

2 pounds leftover baked ham, sliced

4 Yukon Gold potatoes, sliced

½ pound cheddar cheese, shredded

1 quart heavy cream

Salt and pepper to taste

Directions:

Preheat oven to 350 degrees.

In a casserole dish, place an even layer of the ham, followed by an even layer of the sliced potatoes, then an even layer of the cheese. Repeat these layers as many times as necessary to fill the dish.

Season the cream with salt and pepper and pour over the layers. Cover with aluminum foil and bake for 1 hour.

Remove the foil and bake for an additional 30 minutes, or until the top browns and the potatoes are tender when stuck with a fork. Serve hot.

Elysian Fields Farm, Waynesburg, Pennsylvania

Name: Keith Martin

What I do: I raise lamb.

How I got started: I was in the world of finance with a brokerage firm, and I did well, but definitely felt out of my element. When I looked around at the people I admired most, they were all farmers. So I decided to be a farmer too, and thank God my wife supported me 100 percent. Now, every day is an effort, but I don't regret one day of the road that led me here. And I've actually used my business experience to run the farm. But the change came from a very introspective place, something very real.

What my typical day is like: I'm up at 5 a.m. every day, and leave at 5:45 a.m. to go to the processing plant. I'm there all morning and then spend the rest of the afternoon on the farm. Right now we're shearing sheep, bailing hay, mowing pastures. It really all depends on what the weather is doing. You've got to gauge what you do every day according to the forecast. But mostly I'm in the barns; that's where I belong.

What's special about what we do: We focus away from commercialism and shift everything onto the animal. I'm with these animals for their lives, for their slaughter, and sometimes when they're consumed. So I feel it's incumbent upon on me to bring a reverence and respect for the lamb to the chefs who serve them and the people who eat them. The focus has to be on the animal; it can't be on making a buck. We make sure the animal has a good life. They get a wholesome diet, we make sure they get clean bedding, we look at it from a holistic perspective. People who eat our lamb are directly connected to the source in that respect. I love to work with chefs who get that, like Peter Davis.

How I like to eat it all: We love it grilled, with just a little salt and pepper to draw out the flavor. Do that and you're going to eat big. We don't trim away all the fat, because that and the bone shape the flavor of the meat. When you grill something, that's what you get: the truest taste of the animal.

Meatloaf

Serves 6

Ingredients:

½ cup onion, diced

½ cup celery, diced

2 ounces butter

2 eggs, beaten

½ cup milk

½ loaf white bread, toasted, crusts trimmed, and diced

2¼ teaspoons garlic, diced

2¼ teaspoons sea salt

¾ teaspoon black pepper

1½ teaspoons dried basil

2½ pounds ground beef

Directions:

Preheat oven to 350 degrees.

Sweat the onion and the celery in butter, then cool.

Mix the eggs with the milk and add the diced bread.

Combine all remaining ingredients in a separate bowl and mix by hand. Add to the onions and celery mixture, and then combine with eggs, milk, and bread mixture.

Fill a loaf pan with the mixture.

Place the loaf pan in the oven, a ½-inch away from the top and bake until the internal temperature is 165 degrees. Slice and serve.

Venison Sausage with Smoked Bacon Sauerkraut

Serves 6

Ingredients:

4 ounces smoked bacon, diced

12 ounces sauerkraut, drained

2 tablespoons caraway seeds

½ cup Chicken Stock (see page 163)

4 venison sausages

4 rolls

Dijon mustard

Directions:

Sauté the bacon until crispy. Add the sauerkraut, caraway seeds, and Chicken Stock. Reduce to low heat and simmer for 1 hour.

Grill the sausages. Place in a roll and top with sauerkraut. Serve with Dijon mustard.

River Rock Farm Sirloin and Spinach Salad

Serves 4

I urge you to find a local meat purveyor at your farmers' market and try the product. You'll be happy you did.

Ingredients:

4 6-ounce River Rock sirloin steaks

1 teaspoon fresh thyme, chopped

1 teaspoon fresh rosemary, chopped

1 clove garlic, chopped

¼ cup olive oil

Salt and pepper to taste

8 ounces fresh spinach, washed and dried

1 cup roasted Garlic and Cumin Dressing (see page 171)

8 ounces Great Hill blue cheese

Directions:

Marinate the steaks in the herbs, garlic, and oil overnight.

Season the steaks with salt and pepper and grill to desired doneness.

Divide the spinach onto 4 plates.

Slice each steak into 5 pieces and fan out over the plates of spinach.

Drizzle evenly with the dressing and top with crumbled blue cheese. Garnish with tomatoes in season.

Smoked and Grilled Pork Chops

Serves 4

Ingredients:

4 10-ounce responsibly raised pork chops

4 cups Wet Brine (see page 165)

½ cup wood chips

1 cup fresh Applesauce (see page 160)

Directions:

Place the pork chops in the brine and refrigerate overnight.

Remove the chops from the brine.

Soak the wood chips in water for 5 minutes. Drain and loosely wrap in foil.

Place the wood chips on the fire of a covered grill.

When the chips begin to smoke heavily, extinguish the flame and place the chops on a rack over a pan of ice, into the grill. Close the top immediately.

Let the chops smoke for 1 hour.

Remove the chops and ice pan from the grill.

Relight the grill and grill the chops over medium-high heat to desired doneness.

Serve with the Applesauce.

Cider-Braised Pork

Serves 6

Ingredients:

3 pounds boneless pork loin roast

1 quart Wet Brine (see page 165)

1 onion, peeled and cut into eighths

1 stalk celery, cut into 1-inch lengths

1 carrot, cut into 1-inch lengths

2 bay leaves

2 cups apple cider

1 cup Veal or Oxtail Stock (see page 164)

1 cup Chicken Stock (see page 163)

Salt and pepper to taste

Directions:

Soak the pork in the Wet Brine overnight. Remove the pork from the brine.

Place the pork in a heavy-bottomed pot and sear fat-side down first, then on all sides until golden brown.

Remove from the pan and add in the onion, celery, carrot, and bay leaves. Continue to cook until the vegetables are browned.

Add the cider and reduce by half.

Add the pork and the Veal or Oxtail and Chicken stocks to the pan and continue cooking at a slow simmer until the meat has an internal temperature of 165 degrees.

Remove the meat from the pan and let rest 30 minutes before slicing.

Strain the sauce, season with salt and pepper, and pour over the sliced pork.

Chipotle Spiced Pork

Serves 6

Ingredients:

2 pork tenderloins

2 tablespoons store-bought chipotle pepper powder

1½ cups Bourbon BBQ Sauce (see page 162)

2 ounces pale ale beer

Salt and pepper to taste

Directions:

Rub the meat with the chipotle powder and marinate for 2 hours.

Grill over medium heat until it reaches an internal temperature of 160 degrees.

In a saucepot, reduce the beer by half and add the Bourbon BBQ Sauce. Bring to a boil.

Put pork aside to rest for 15 minutes before slicing. Top with the sauce.

Maple Stout-Marinated Beef Brisket

Serves 8

This flavorful and filling dinner is excellent with mashed potatoes.

Ingredients:

1 4-pound beef brisket

4 cups Maple Stout Marinade (see page 167)

Directions:

Soak the brisket in the marinade for 24 hours.

Remove the brisket from the marinade and grill over low heat to brown on all sides, being careful not to burn.

Remove from the grill and put in a pan on a rack and cover tightly.

Preheat oven to 275 degrees.

Place the brisket in the oven and cook for 6 hours, removing the top and basting with the marinade every hour.

When the brisket is tender, remove from the oven and let rest lightly covered for 30 minutes.

Slice the brisket thinly across the grain and drizzle with the pan drippings.

River Rock Farm, Brimfield, Massachusetts

Name: Ron Konove

What I raise: Pasture-raised, all-natural beef.

How I got started: My son was finishing college and got admitted to medical school nine years ago. We had a few cows, and he decided to defer school for a year to try working on the farm. Well, we kept getting more and more cattle, and our meat went over really well. So he decided to defer a second year, and we expanded and kept adding new markets. Then he put school off again, and then it just took off. Now we sell in western Massachusetts. We ship everywhere, we do home deliveries, and sell to select restaurants.

What's special about what we do: We have a custom feed, but mostly we buy the right animals and take care of them, and keep them happy. We also dry-age our meats, which is something most people don't do because it's very expensive. But the resulting flavor is incredible. It's a balancing act—an art form, because every carcass is different, and if you age it too much it dries out.

How to pick a great steak: Look for some fat marbling in the piece you're buying, but different cuts have more or less fat in them, and there's a lot of variation. I think even a plain old hamburger can be an incredible way to eat beef, and it's very different than other kinds like stew meat. Likewise, a dry-aged steak looks different than a grass-fed product. But the ultimate test of any cut is the taste.

My favorite way to eat it all: We don't grill that much, because we do most of our meat cooking in a cast-iron pan. We like minimum seasoning; that way you can sear and seal in the flavor, and finish it off under the broiler. I could probably eat our hamburger every day. And I love the brisket and the short ribs, too, which are just amazing.

Rack of Venison

Serves 8

Ingredients:

2 tablespoons whole
black peppercorns

6 juniper berries

2 bay leaves

1 8-bone venison rack, frenched

2 stalks celery

1 carrot

1 onion

Red Wine Sauce (see page 162)

Directions:

Crush the peppercorns, juniper, and bay leaves, and sprinkle over the venison.

Place the venison into a casserole dish.

Wash the celery and carrot and roughly chop into ¼-inch slices.

Peel the onion, cut in half, and cut into ¼-inch slices.

Cover the venison with vegetables, cover the casserole, and marinate for 2 days, refrigerated.

Remove the venison from the casserole dish and wipe off the vegetables, setting them aside.

Sear the venison to brown on all sides.

Preheat oven to 350 degrees.

Place the venison in a roasting pan with the vegetables from the marinade and place in the oven.

Cook until venison reaches an internal temperature of 125 degrees and remove from the oven.

Let the rack stand for 20 minutes, lightly covered.

Cut the venison into 8 chops, slicing next to each bone. Serve with Red Wine Sauce.

Beef and Pork Chili

Serves 6

To make this classic chili hotter, add cayenne pepper to taste.

Ingredients:

2 pounds beef stew meat

1 pound pork stew meat

Salt and pepper to taste

3 medium onions, chopped

4 cloves garlic, chopped

3 tablespoons vegetable oil

2 chipotle peppers

2 cups canned whole tomatoes

4 dried ancho peppers

2 tablespoons chili powder

2 teaspoons cumin

2 bay leaves

8 ounces pale ale beer

1 cup Chicken Stock (see page 163)

Cayenne pepper, if desired

Directions:

Season the meat with salt and pepper and grill over high heat to a char. Remove from the grill.

Sauté the onions and garlic in the oil until golden. Add the meat and remaining ingredients and cook until the meat is tender and the sauce is reduced.

Pot Roast

Serves 6

Mashed potatoes are the perfect partner for this stick-to-your-ribs classic.

Ingredients:

1 4-pound piece of chuck

Salt and pepper

4 tablespoons vegetable oil

3 cloves garlic

2 carrots, roughly chopped

3 celery sticks, roughly chopped

1 medium onion, peeled and chopped

1 cup red wine

3 cups Veal or Oxtail Stock (see page 164)

2 bay leaves

2 sprigs fresh thyme

Directions:

Preheat oven to 350 degrees.

Season the chuck with salt and pepper.

Place a heavy-bottomed pot on the stove over medium heat. Add the oil and brown the chuck on all sides. Remove the chuck from the pot and set aside.

Add the garlic, carrot, celery, and onion and brown well.

Pour the red wine into the pot and reduce by half.

Add the meat, stock, bay leaves, and thyme into the pot, and bring to a boil. Place the uncovered pot into the oven.

Cook the roast for 2½ hours, turning every half hour. If the sauce reduces too much and becomes too thick, add 1 cup water.

Remove the pot roast from the oven when it is fork-tender.

Remove the meat from the pot and set aside.

Skim the fat off the top of the sauce. Puree the sauce and season with salt and pepper.

Slice the meat across the grain, top with sauce, and serve.

Poultry

Henrietta's Table Chicken Potpie

Serves 6 to 8

Ingredients:

For the filling:

¼ cup butter

¼ cup flour

2 cups cold Chicken Stock
(see page 163)

⅓ cup pearl onions, peeled

1 cup celery, diced

1 cup carrot, diced

½ cup peas

Salt and pepper to taste

For the potpie:

1 pound cooked chicken meat, white,
dark, or a combination of both

8 ounces H.T. Daily Pie dough
(see page 197)

1 egg

Directions:

Preheat oven to 350 degrees.

Heat the butter over low heat and stir in the flour. Cook for 5 minutes, stirring to prevent burning.

Whisk in the cold Chicken Stock and bring to a boil.

Add in the onions, celery, and carrot, and cook at a low simmer until the vegetables are tender. Add the peas.

Season with salt and pepper, and set aside.

Layer the chicken into a pottery crock. Cover with filling.

Roll the pie dough flat, and cover the top of the crock. Trim edges and cut a small vent on top.

Beat the egg and apply to the top of the crust with a pastry brush.

Bake for 45 minutes, or until internal temperature is 165 degrees. Serve hot.

Misty Knoll Farm, New Haven, Vermont

Name: Rob Litch

What I raise: Poultry—meaning chicken and turkey.

How I got started: Actually, it was a 4-H project more than 20 years ago. My partner's daughter was in the organization and decided she wanted to grow turkeys in the basement of their house. When we were done, everyone commented on their amazing flavor, and so we decided to grow more, and then kept growing more and more up until the present day. Now it's myself, my uncle, and his son.

What my average day is like: That's just not possible to describe; every day is a little different. Some days we catch chickens, some days we process them, some days we do bookkeeping. It's always different.

What's special about what we do: We continue to produce food for our family, it's just that our family happens to include all of our customers these days. Our turkeys are free-range, and on an all-natural diet. The chickens are raised without antibiotics and are fed no animal products. They're raised cage-free, in a barn (referred to by some as free-roaming). We grow stuff the best way we can while producing the best products for our customers and maintaining our personal integrity. All of the above, plus high-quality feed and the freshness affect the flavor of our poultry. You can taste the difference on the first bite.

My favorite way to eat it all: I love to take the leftovers and make soup out of them. I just love soup—and it gives you the opportunity to use up a lot of stuff in your fridge, and a lot of local ingredients. I find that very rewarding.

Grilled Chicken Salad with Walnuts and Grapes on a Bed of Romaine

Serves 10

Ingredients:

4 pounds chicken breast

2 tablespoons Chicken Herbs (see page 167)

1 tablespoon garlic, chopped

2 tablespoons olive oil

1 cup celery, diced

1 cup red onion, diced

1 cup red grapes, halved

½ cup toasted walnut halves, crushed

2 cups mayonnaise

6 tablespoons whole grain mustard

1 teaspoon Worcestershire sauce

Salt and pepper to taste

2 heads romaine lettuce

Directions:

Season chicken with Chicken Herbs, garlic, and olive oil, and grill until cooked through. Cool, then dice.

Mix all ingredients together and serve over washed and cut romaine lettuce.

Roasted Turkey

Serves 8

Ingredients:

1 gallon Wet Brine (see page 165)

1 10-pound turkey

10 fresh sage leaves

2 stalks celery

2 medium-sized carrots

3 medium-sized onions, peeled

4 tablespoons olive oil

Salt and pepper

½ cup butter, melted

⅓ cup Vermont maple syrup

Directions:

Soak the turkey in the Wet Brine overnight.

Preheat oven to 450 degrees.

Remove the turkey from the brine and pat dry. Lift the skin on the breast and evenly distribute the sage leaves under it by gently separating the skin from the center of the bird halves, leaving the sides attached, and inserting the leaves.

Wash the celery and carrots and chop into 1-inch cubes, repeat with the onion.

Rub the turkey with olive oil and sprinkle lightly with salt and pepper.

Place the vegetables in a roasting pan and place the turkey above them on a rack on the top rack in the oven for 30 minutes. Turn the oven down to 325 degrees and roast for 1 more hour.

Mix the butter and the maple syrup together. Use the mixture to baste the turkey frequently while roasting for the last hour, or until the thickest part of the breast reaches a temperature of 165 degrees.

Remove the turkey from the oven and let rest 30 minutes before slicing and serving.

Chicken 2 Ways

Serves 6

This dish is great with mashed potatoes or au gratin potatoes.

Ingredients:

3 2½-pound free-range chickens

Salt and pepper

4 tablespoons olive oil

½ cup celery, diced

1 cup onion, diced

½ cup carrot, diced

4 cloves garlic, chopped

3 cups red wine

2 quarts dark Chicken Demi-glace (see page 168)

2 bay leaves

2 sprigs rosemary

2 sprigs thyme

Directions:

Remove the breasts from the chickens by cutting off at the breast bone, keeping the wing intact.

Cover and refrigerate.

Remove the legs from the carcass and split them in the joint, between the drumstick and the thigh. (This may be done up to 2 days in advance.)

Season the legs with salt and pepper and sear in 2 tablespoons of olive oil over medium-high heat, browning on all sides.

Remove from the pan and add the vegetables and garlic and sauté until golden brown.

Add the wine and reduce by half.

Add the Chicken Demi-glace, herbs, and chicken. Bring to a boil and reduce the heat to a slow simmer.

Cook until the chicken is fork-tender, about 45 minutes to 1 hour.

Remove the chicken from the sauce and cool.

Strain the sauce, defat and cool.

For the dish:

Preheat oven to 320 degrees.

Season the breasts with salt and pepper and sauté over medium heat in 2 tablespoons of olive oil, browning on both sides.

Place on a rack in oven and cook to an internal temperature of 165 degrees (about 45 minutes).

Remove from the oven and let rest for 10 minutes before slicing.

In the meantime, reheat the braised legs in the sauce to 165 degrees.

Slice the breasts into 4 slices each.

Arrange the legs and breasts on a plate and cover with the sauce.

Duck Confit and Maple-Brined Breast

Serves 6

Ingredients:

1 teaspoon fennel
seed, ground

½ teaspoon red pepper flakes,
ground

2 cups Dry Brine (see page 165)

6 duck legs

6 duck breasts

2 cups Maple Wet Brine (see
page 165)

½ pint duck fat

Red Wine Sauce (see page 162)

Fruit compote of your choice

Directions:

Mix the fennel seed and red pepper flakes with the Dry Brine and cover the duck legs with the mix. Refrigerate for 12 hours.

Soak the breasts in the Maple Wet Brine. Refrigerate for 12 hours.

For the confit legs:

Preheat oven to 250 degrees.

Remove the duck legs from the refrigerator and brush off the brine.

Place the legs in a heavy pan with the duck fat and cover.

Place the pan into oven and cook for 3½ to 4 hours, or until the meat is very soft.

Remove from the oven, uncover, and let cool in the fat. (The confit may be made up to 1 week in advance and stored refrigerated in the fat.)

For the breasts:

Preheat oven to 250 degrees.

Remove the breasts from the brine.

Pat the breasts dry and sear in a well-heated pan, skin-side down until the skin is crispy and golden brown.

Turn over and repeat.

Place the seared breasts in the oven and cook to a 125-degree internal temperature.

Remove from the oven and let rest for 5 minutes before slicing.

To reheat, remove the legs from the fat and place on a sheet pan in the oven for 15 to 20 minutes.

Serve the breast and leg together with Red Wine Sauce and fruit compote.

Grilled Chicken Breast
with Apple Cider Reduction

I love to serve this sweet-and-savory dish with potatoes (mashed or au gratin) and caramelized cauliflower.

Ingredients:

4 chicken breasts

4 tablespoons Chicken Herbs (see page 167)

1 clove garlic, chopped

¾ cup olive oil

4 cups apple cider

1 star anise

2 pieces whole allspice

1 clove

½ orange

Directions:

Place the chicken in a bowl with the herbs, garlic, and half of the oil and marinate overnight.

Preheat oven to 300 degrees.

In a saucepan, place the cider, star anise, allspice, clove, and orange and bring to a boil.

Reduce by two-thirds and strain. Keep at room temperature.

In a skillet, heat the remaining oil and sear the chicken over medium-high heat, skin side first, until crispy and golden brown.

Flip the chicken and repeat.

Remove the chicken from the skillet and place on a rack in the oven and cook to an internal temperature of 165 degrees (approximately 20 to 25 minutes).

Herb~Crusted Rotisserie Chicken

Serves 6

If you don't have a rotisserie at your disposal, you can use a conventional oven instead. Just roast the chicken at 350 degrees and it comes out delicious.

Ingredients:

3 whole free-range chickens

Chicken Mustard (see page 167)

Chicken Herbs (see page 167)

Directions:

Wash the chickens in cold running water and pat dry with a towel.

Truss the chicken.

Coat the entire chicken with the mustard (patting to coat evenly) and then coat with the herbs.

Skewer and cook the chickens on the rotisserie until the internal temperature of the thigh is 165 degrees (about 2½ hours, depending on rotisserie temperature).

Remove the chickens from the rotisserie and let rest for 30 minutes.

Carve the chickens and serve.

Jurgielwicz Farm, Moriches, New York

Name: Tom Jurgielwicz

What I do: I raise ducks.

How I got started: I'm third generation. My grandparents came from Poland through Ellis Island, and started raising ducks in eastern Long Island. Then my dad did it, and now it's myself and my brother. I took a break to go college, then decided to come right back to the farm.

My typical day: I'm usually out on the farm with the ducks. We hatch them, grow them, and process them. We grow about a million-and-a-quarter to a million-and-a-half ducks a year.

What's special about what we do: Right now there are five operations raising white Peking ducks in the United States, and we're the last one raising them free-range. We have hand-selected markets: the upper-end white tablecloth restaurants, the Chinese restaurant market in the States, and then we're also the only farm with kosher ducks.

How to pick them: You should be able to look at the duck and see unblemished skin. You want to get a nice and crisp skin that doesn't rip or tear when you cook it, and only ducks that are free-range, that have had access to swim water, get that. That's because when they swim, they preen themselves, which creates great oily skin glands and results in an oilier skin that cooks much better.

My favorite way to eat it all: The way any great chef cooks it: I love duck confit. And a great pan-seared duck breast. And I love bringing duck home from Chinatown. I simply love duck. I must eat it four times a week, minimum.

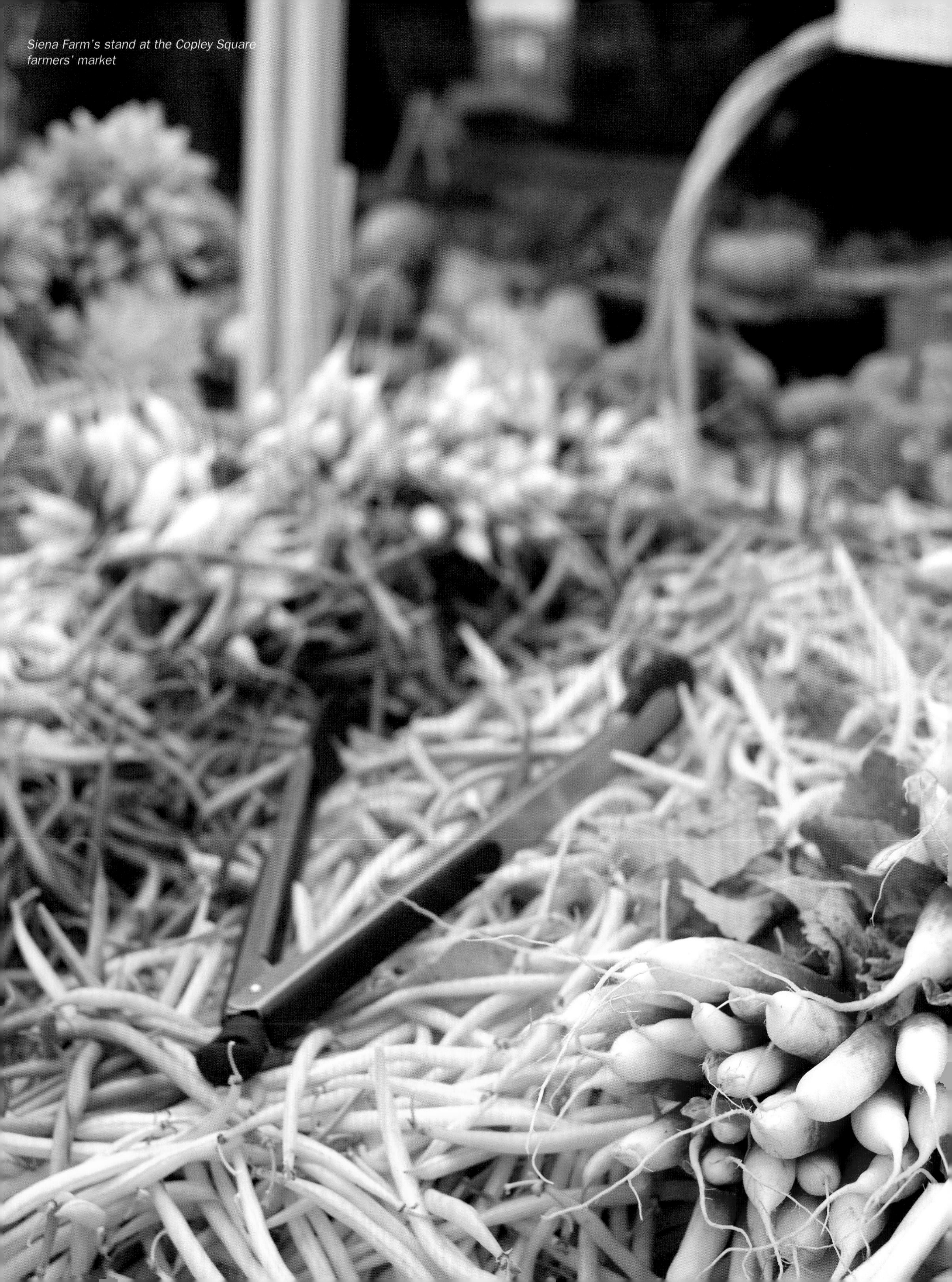

Siena Farm's stand at the Copley Square farmers' market

Sides & Other Stuff

Succotash

They may not be the stars of the show, but in any great movie or play, the performances of supporting characters can make all the difference. The same goes for side dishes in creating the overall effect of a dish: The creaminess of mac 'n' cheese can be the perfect foil for a salty-sweet pork chop. The sweetness of caramelized cauliflower is the ultimate companion to crispy roasted chicken. And is there any better match for a juicy, slightly tangy Porterhouse steak than rich mashed potatoes?

All of that's equally true of condiments, sauces, stocks, brines, and other flavor enhancers. A spice-laden chutney can change the flavor of grilled chicken with just one spoonful. A well-brined pork tenderloin has the kind of velvety texture and deeply embedded flavor that you'll remember for weeks.

In making all of the following recipes, feel free to mix and match them with any of the suggested sides for main dishes throughout this book. This is the essence of the experience that diners have at Henrietta's Table. We love to let diners choose their own pairings; this is where you can get creative. And one of the best parts is that, while some of these basics take more time to prepare than others, most can be made ahead, so the process of getting the food straight from the stove to the table is that much more direct.

Succotash

Serves 8

Ingredients:

2 cups dried lima beans

6 ears fresh corn

½ cup onion, diced

¼ cup olive oil

Salt and pepper to taste

¼ cup chives, chopped

Directions:

Soak the beans overnight and drain.

Shuck the corn and remove kernels from the cobs, setting kernels aside.

Place the corn cobs in a saucepot and just cover with water. Simmer for 1 hour. Strain, and reserve the stock.

Sauté the onion in the oil until transparent. Add the beans and the corn stock.

Bring to a boil and reduce to a simmer, cooking covered until the beans are tender. Add water if they begin to cook dry.

Add the corn kernels and turn the heat to high, cooking an additional 5 to 6 minutes.

Remove from the heat. Season with salt and pepper and add the chives.

Grilled Asparagus

Serves 6

Ingredients:

1½ pounds fresh medium-thick asparagus

1 lemon

2 ounces olive or salad oil

Salt and pepper

Directions:

Trim the asparagus and peel if tough.

Zest the lemon using a potato peeler, being careful to only take off the yellow skin.

Chop the zest very fine and mix with the oil.

Toss the asparagus in the oil and season with salt and pepper.

Grill over medium heat, turning occasionally to prevent burning, and remove from the heat when tender.

Squeeze the juice from half of the lemon over the asparagus and serve warm or at room temperature.

Oven-Roasted Root Vegetables

Serves 4

Ingredients:

½ pound parsnips

½ pound rutabaga, peeled

½ pound purple top turnip

½ pound celeriac

½ pound carrots

2 ounces butter, melted

Salt and pepper

Directions:

Preheat oven to 350 degrees.

Cut all vegetables into 1-inch cubes.

Place vegetables into a bowl and toss with the melted butter. Add salt and pepper to taste.

Place on a flat baking tray and roast for approximately 30 minutes, or until the vegetables are tender.

Wilted Spinach

Serves 4

Ingredients:

1 teaspoon garlic, chopped

½ teaspoon fresh ginger, chopped

2 tablespoons olive oil

2 ounces spinach

¼ cup water

Salt and pepper

Directions:

Sauté the garlic and ginger in the oil for 1 minute over medium heat.

Add the spinach and water and cook until the spinach is tender.

Season with salt and pepper.

Brussels Sprouts

Serves 8

Ingredients:

2 pounds Brussels sprouts

½ pound applewood smoked bacon

Directions:

Preheat oven to 350 degrees.

Clean the sprouts by removing the outer leaves and cutting an X in the trimmed stem, approximately ⅛-inch deep.

Blanch the sprouts in salted boiling water until tender and shock in ice water to cool and retain color.

Cut the bacon in a medium dice and sauté in a cast-iron skillet until it is about halfway cooked.

Add the drained sprouts and toss with the bacon. Place the pan in the oven and cook until heated through.

Creamed Onions

Serves 4

Ingredients:

1 pound fresh cipollini or pearl onions

2 cups heavy cream

¼ cup aged local cheese, freshly grated

Salt and pepper to taste

Directions:

Peel the onions by placing them in boiling water for 2 minutes, then cool them in ice water immediately.

Place the onions in a heavy-bottomed saucepan, cover with the cream, and bring to a boil.

Reduce to a simmer and cook uncovered, until the onions are soft (about 1 to 1½ hours).

Preheat broiler.

Stir in the cheese to melt and season with salt and pepper. Place onions in the broiler to brown. Serve immediately.

Caramelized Cauliflower

Serves 4

Ingredients:

1 head cauliflower

4 tablespoons extra virgin olive oil

Salt and pepper to taste

Directions:

Preheat oven to 450 degrees.

Clean the cauliflower into large, bite-sized florets by removing the leaves and core.

Toss the florets with the oil, salt, and pepper, and spread into a cast-iron skillet.

Roast the cauliflower in the oven until it is cooked through (approximately 30 minutes) and lightly browned.

Baked Carrots

Serves 8

Ingredients:

8 carrots, peeled

1 teaspoon maple syrup

¼ cup orange juice

8 teaspoons maple sugar

Directions:

Preheat oven to 350 degrees.

Wrap carrots, maple syrup, orange juice, and maple sugar in aluminum foil, creating a tight seal.

Place in the oven for 30 minutes or until carrots are tender.

Roasted Beets

Makes 1 batch

These beets are excellent alone or tossed in a little butter and chopped tarragon.

Ingredients:

1 pound beets, each about the size of a golf ball, greens removed

2 tablespoons olive oil

2 tablespoons salt

Directions:

Preheat oven to 350 degrees.

Wash the beets thoroughly.

Rub the beets with the oil, then the salt.

Place the beets on a cookie sheet in the oven for 45 minutes or until a skewer pokes through them smoothly.

Remove from the oven and let stand until cool to the touch.

Using a towel, rub the skin from the beets. Wash the beets with water to remove any small pieces of skin.

Reheat the beets in the oven when ready to serve.

Wilted Greens

Serves 6

Ingredients:

½ pound fresh spinach

½ pound Swiss chard

½ pound beet greens

½ pound mustard greens

½ pound Tuscan kale

2 teaspoons garlic, chopped

2 teaspoons shallots or red onion, chopped

4 teaspoons olive oil

½ cup water

Salt and pepper

Directions:

Trim all the greens and cut into 3-inch pieces.

Wash all the greens thoroughly in cold water and mix together. Drain well.

Over medium heat, sauté the garlic and shallots or red onion in the oil.

Add the greens and the water and sauté, stirring constantly to cook the greens evenly.

When the greens are wilted, season with salt and pepper, and remove from the pan with tongs, leaving the juices behind.

Butternut Squash Puree

Serves 4

Ingredients:

1 medium-sized fresh butternut squash

4 tablespoons butter

⅛ cup maple syrup

Salt and pepper to taste

Directions:

Peel the squash, cut it in half lengthwise, and deseed.

Cut the squash into a 2-inch dice.

Steam the squash until soft but not mushy (about 30 minutes). Place the squash in an uncovered bowl and let sit for 5 minutes.

Mash the squash with an electric beater or hand potato masher until smooth.

Mix in the butter and maple syrup and season with salt and pepper.

Macaroni and Cheese

Serves 4

Ingredients:

4 tablespoons melted butter

4 tablespoons all-purpose flour

1 pint cold milk

1 pint cold light cream

½ cup sharp cheddar, grated

½ cup smoked cheddar, grated

1 dash Tabasco sauce

Salt and pepper to taste

4 cups macaroni, cooked

¼ cup coarse dried
bread crumbs

Directions:

Preheat oven to 350 degrees.

Make a roux by heating the melted butter in a pan over low heat and whisking in the flour.

Cook the mixture for 5 minutes, stirring occasionally. Then whisk in the milk and cream to dissolve the roux.

Increase the heat to medium and bring the mixture to a boil. Reduce the heat and simmer for 30 minutes, stirring to prevent scorching.

Fold in both cheeses and continue to cook until they are melted and thoroughly incorporated. Remove from the heat and season with Tabasco and salt and pepper.

Mix the macaroni with the sauce and pour into an ovenproof casserole dish. Sprinkle the top with the bread crumbs and place the casserole in the oven. Cook until the internal temperature reaches 350 degrees and the top is golden brown. Serve hot.

Henrietta's Table Mashed Potatoes

Serves 4

The secret to this incredible version is in the process; the timing must be exact to produce potatoes that are both rich and light in texture.

Ingredients:

2 pounds potatoes, peeled (approximately 5 large russet potatoes)

¼ pound butter, cut into cubes

⅓ cup milk

Salt and pepper to taste

Directions:

Cook potatoes in boiling water for approximately 45 minutes. Be sure not to overcook them.

Drain potatoes and let them steam dry for about 5 to 6 minutes.

Place potatoes in a mixing bowl and use a paddle to mix. Mix without milk or butter until smooth, approximately 1 minute.

Add butter and mix well.

Add milk and season with salt and pepper to taste. Do not overmix or the potatoes will be pasty.

Maple Baked Beans

Serves 10

Ingredients:

1 pound heirloom beans, soaked overnight

½ pound bacon ends or salt pork

½ of 1 onion, chopped

1 clove

1 bay leaf

1 teaspoon chili flakes

1 cup maple syrup

3 teaspoons extra virgin olive oil

Directions:

Preheat oven to 250 degrees.

Cover beans by 2 times in water in a saucepan and bring to a boil. Strain.

Now mix the beans and remaining ingredients in the pan, cover with water as necessary and bring to a boil.

Cook mixture until tender in the oven in a saucepan (about 4 hours) or in a clay bean pot (about 6 hours), adding water just to cover as necessary.

Nana's Baked Beans

Serves 6

This was a specialty of my mother's when I was growing up. It is best served with hot dogs and brown bread.

Ingredients:

1 pound small white beans

2 ounces salt pork

1 small onion, chopped

½ teaspoon prepared mustard

⅓ cup brown mustard

⅓ cup molasses

Directions:

Preheat oven to 250 degrees.

Soak the beans overnight in cold water.

Drain and rinse the beans, cover with cold water in a pot, and bring to a boil. Cook until the skins on the beans crack.

Put all the ingredients, except the beans, in a clay bean pot and mix thoroughly.

Add the beans and cover with boiling water. Bake for 8 hours, adding water as necessary.

Goat Cheese Polenta Cake

Serves 8

Ingredients:

½ cup onions, diced small

½ tablespoon extra virgin olive oil

6 cups water

2 cups fresh ground polenta

8 ounces fresh goat cheese

¼ cup chives, chopped fine

Salt and pepper to taste

Directions:

Sweat onions in oil until transparent, add water, and bring to a boil.

Whisk in the polenta and cook over medium to low heat for 40 minutes.

Remove from heat, whisk in cheese, chives, and salt and pepper, spread evenly on half-sheet pans and cool.

Celery Root Potatoes

Serves 4

Ingredients:

1 cup celery root, peeled and diced

2 cups milk

6 medium Idaho potatoes, peeled

¼ pound butter

Salt and pepper

Directions:

Place the celery root and milk in a pot and boil until the celery root is tender.

Remove from the heat and blend to a puree.

Cook the potatoes in boiling, salted water, strain, and let them steam dry for 5 minutes.

Mash the potatoes, add the butter and celery root puree, and season with salt and pepper.

Blue Cheese au Gratin Potatoes

Serves 4

These are a favorite at home with grilled or roasted meat, game or poultry.

Ingredients:

4 russet potatoes

¾ cup Great Hill blue cheese (or any creamy blue)

Salt and pepper

1 pint heavy cream

Directions:

Preheat oven to 350 degrees.

Slice the washed potatoes in ¼-inch thick slices.

Arrange the potatoes in a cast-iron pan (or ovenproof casserole) in at least 3 layers, alternating each layer with the blue cheese and salt and pepper.

Bring the cream to a boil and pour over the potatoes. Cover the pan with plastic film and foil.

Place the pan in the oven (put a cookie sheet underneath in case the cream boils over). Cook for 45 minutes, or until the potatoes are tender when stuck with a fork and the cream has reduced. Remove cover and cook for 10 minutes to brown top.

Remove from the oven and cool for 15 minutes before serving.

Buttermilk Biscuits

Serves 6

Ingredients:

2¼ cups all-purpose flour

1½ tablespoons sugar

4 teaspoons baking powder

½ teaspoon salt

1 cup butter, diced and chilled

1½ cups buttermilk

Directions:

Preheat oven to 350 degrees.

In a large bowl, mix together the flour, sugar, baking powder, and salt.

Cut up butter into small pieces, then add to bowl of dry ingredients in pieces and mix until the mixture reaches a sandy texture.

Add in buttermilk and mix until a dough forms.

Take dough out of bowl and lightly knead on a floured surface. Fold repeatedly onto itself to create layers for 1 minute.

Pat dough out to a 3-inch thickness. Either with a circular cutter or using a knife freehand, cut out biscuits to the desired size.

Bake for 10 to 15 minutes until golden brown.

Sugar Pumpkin Slaw

Serves 6

Ingredients:

1 small sugar pumpkin

½ head cabbage

⅔ cup dried cherries

Creamy Peppercorn Dressing
(see page 172) to taste

Directions:

Peel and seed pumpkin. Shred the meat in an electric food processor or by hand.

Slice cabbage very thinly.

Mix all ingredients, and add dressing to taste.

Pickled Apples

Serves 6

Ingredients:

½ cup sugar

½ cup apple cider vinegar

1 cinnamon stick, broken in half

3 cloves

4 pieces whole allspice

½ cup water

2 pounds apples, halved, cored, and sliced thin

2 tablespoons crystallized ginger, julienned

Directions:

Combine sugar, vinegar, and spices in a medium saucepan. Add water and bring to a boil.

Stir until sugar dissolves. Reduce heat and simmer 10 minutes.

Remove from heat and pour the warm liquid over apples. Add the ginger and refrigerate overnight.

Kosher Dill Pickles

Makes 1 gallon

*Depending on how you like your pickles, you can swap the red chilis
below for habañeros or jalapeños to turn up the heat.
Add cauliflower, carrots, beans, and onions, if you like.*

Ingredients:

4 quarts medium-sized pickling
cucumbers

1 quart vinegar

½ cup kosher salt

3 quarts water

6 stems fresh dill

6 cloves garlic, crushed

6 hot red chili peppers

Directions:

Wash the cucumbers and let stand in the
refrigerator overnight in water.

Bring the vinegar, salt, and water to a boil.

Combine the cucumbers, dill, garlic, and
peppers in a stainless steel or glass container
and pour the boiling liquid over them.

Store in a refrigerator for 1 week
before serving.

Flageolet Bean Salad

Serves 4

Ingredients:

1 red pepper

2 ears corn, roasted

1 pound fresh flageolet beans, hulled

½ red onion, diced

1 carrot, diced

1½ stalks celery, diced

2 yellow tomatoes

¼ cup tarragon, chopped

1½ cloves garlic, chopped

4 tablespoons cider vinegar

¾ cup extra virgin olive oil

3 dashes Tabasco sauce

Salt and pepper to taste

Directions:

Preheat oven to 350 degrees.

Roast the red pepper on the top rack, turning after each side turns black, until it is mostly black all around. Let cool.

Skin the pepper, remove the seeds inside, and dice.

Shuck the corn and roast it in the oven for 15 minutes. Cut the kernels off the cob.

Cook beans in lightly salted, simmering water until tender. Set aside to cool.

Combine all ingredients and serve either warm or cold.

Roasted Spicy Apples

Serves 6

Ingredients:

6 Cortland apples, cored and cut into eighths

¼ cup safflower oil

¼ teaspoon cloves

¼ teaspoon cinnamon

Salt and pepper

Directions:

Preheat oven to 400 degrees.

Toss everything together in a bowl and spread evenly on a sheet pan.

Place sheet pan in the oven and bake for 10 to 12 minutes.

Mustard Pickles

Serves 6

Ingredients:

1¼ pounds cucumber, peeled

⅝ pound white onions, diced

1¼ stalks celery, diced

½ of 1 large red pepper, diced

⅛ head cauliflower, diced

1¼ tablespoons mustard powder

1¾ teaspoons mustard seed

2⅔ teaspoons celery seed

2 whole cloves

2 cups water

3 cups white vinegar

½ cup honey

½ teaspoon turmeric

2⅜ tablespoons salt

Directions:

Peel and seed cucumbers and dice in ½-inches. Dice onion, celery, and red pepper in ½-inches.

Break cauliflower into small, equally-sized florets. Sauté the mustard powder and seed, celery seed, and cloves for 1 minute in a little oil.

Add water, vinegar, honey, turmeric, and salt. Bring liquid to a boil and add the vegetables. Take off the heat and let cool.

Mushroom Ketchup

Makes 4 cups

Ingredients:

1 pound mushrooms (any variety), sliced

1 tablespoon salt

4 Roma tomatoes, halved, roasted, and skin removed

1¼ cups red wine vinegar

1½ teaspoons allspice

¼-inch fresh ginger, chopped

1 blade mace

½ of 1 shallot, chopped

Directions:

Soak mushrooms in salt for 2 days, stirring occasionally to coat.

Preheat oven to 350 degrees.

Roast tomatoes on a rack in the oven for 30 minutes.

Place all ingredients in a pot with a heavy bottom and cook over low heat until mushrooms are tender.

Puree and cool. Serve with grilled meats or vegetables.

Smoked Tomato Ketchup

Serves 10

*If you don't want to smoke the tomatoes, you can also char them
on your grill on very high heat, creating grill marks all over.*

Ingredients:

3 pounds Roma tomatoes, smoked

2 cups white onions, diced

¼ cup cider vinegar

¼ cup brown sugar

1¼ teaspoons allspice

1¼ teaspoons black pepper

1¼ teaspoons salt

2 bay leaves

Directions:

In a smoker, smoke the tomatoes.

Place all ingredients in a pot and cook on medium heat, uncovered, until it
turns to a ketchup-like consistency.

Remove and pulse in food processor until chunky. Refrigerate until ready to use.

Dried Stone Fruit Relish

Makes 1 batch

Ingredients:

1 cup shallots, sliced thinly

½ cup dried cranberries

½ cup dried currants

½ cup golden raisins

½ cup dried prunes

½ cup dried apricots

½ cup dried cherries

¼ cup brown sugar

1 bay leaf

¼ cup Myers dark rum

½ cup orange juice

Directions:

In a medium saucepan, sauté the shallots, add dried fruits, sugar, bay leaf,
and rum.

Cook until alcohol is evaporated and add orange juice. Reduce by half.
Remove from heat and cool.

Cranberry Chutney

Makes 1 batch

This tart, spicy add-on is terrific served with roasted duck.

Ingredients:

1 tablespoon fresh ginger, finely chopped

3 tablespoon shallots, finely chopped

2 teaspoons vegetable oil

1 cinnamon stick

2 pieces star anise

4 cups fresh cranberries

1 cup kumquats, thinly sliced

2 cups fresh orange juice

½ cup sugar

½ cup red wine vinegar

Directions:

In a heavy bottomed saucepan, lightly sauté the ginger and shallots in the oil.

Tie the cinnamon stick and anise in a cheesecloth pouch. Add it, plus the remaining ingredients, to the saucepan.

Bring everything to a boil, then reduce to a simmer and cook, stirring occasionally to prevent sticking, until the cranberries are soft and cooked through.

Set aside to cool.

Apple Chutney

Makes 8 ounces

Ingredients:

1 teaspoon mustard seed

1 clove

⅛ teaspoon chili flakes

3 teaspoons safflower oil

¼ cup onions, diced

1 teaspoon fresh ginger, chopped

3 Granny Smith apples, diced ¼-inch

½ lemon, zested

⅛ teaspoon cinnamon

⅛ teaspoon cardamom

⅛ teaspoon pepper

½ teaspoon salt

2 teaspoons cider vinegar

2 tablespoons apple cider

2 tablespoons honey

Directions:

In a medium saucepan, toast mustard seed, clove, and chili flakes in oil for 3 minutes.

Add onion and ginger and cook until transparent.

Add remaining ingredients and cook over low heat for 30 minutes.

Apricot and Tomato Chutney

Serves 8

Ingredients:

1 ¼ teaspoons cumin seed

1 ¼ teaspoons fennel seed

1 ¼ teaspoons black mustard seed

⅓ teaspoon fenugreek seed

2 tablespoons vegetable oil

½ teaspoon red chili flakes

2 cloves garlic, minced

2 tablespoons fresh ginger, minced

1 pound tomatoes, seeded, peeled, and diced

1 cup sugar

½ cup dried apricot halves

½ cup white vinegar

Directions:

Fry first 4 spices in vegetable oil until crisp.

Add the rest of the ingredients except for the apricots and vinegar. Simmer for 30 minutes.

Add dried apricots and vinegar and simmer for 20 to 30 minutes. Serve at room temperature or chilled, with pork, chicken, or fish.

Strawberry Rhubarb Compote

Serves 10

Ingredients:

3 tablespoons sugar

2 tablespoons mustard seed, toasted

3 pints strawberries, quartered

1 pound rhubarb, peeled and diced

Directions:

In a saucepan over low heat, stir the sugar with the mustard seed until it is lightly caramelized.

Add in the strawberries and rhubarb and cook until fruit is tender. Remove from heat and cool.

Serve cold.

Preserved Lemons

Makes 1 batch

Ingredients:

10 lemons

1 cup kosher salt

2 cups fresh lemon juice

1 sterilized canning jar

Directions:

Trim the tips off of the lemons.

Place 2 tablespoons of the salt in the bottom of the jar.

Cut the lemons in half lengthwise, cutting 90 percent of the way through. Then rotate the lemon and cut the same way to make 4 joined quarters.

Pull open the lemons and sprinkle generously with salt.

Pack the lemons in the jar and press down to extract the juice.

Pour in the additional lemon juice, enough to cover the lemons, and top with remaining salt.

Seal the jar and let sit at room temperature for 3 days, turning upside down daily.

Place in the refrigerator and turn daily for 3 weeks, or until the lemon rinds soften.

Angelini Farming Trust, Wenham, Massachusetts

Name: Pio Angelini

What I make: Primarily berries—blueberries, blackberries, and raspberries.

How I got started: My father and uncle bought this farm in 1938, and grew strawberries. My mother and father left it to me, and I kept it going. My wife is retired and so am I, so we can dedicate more time to growing. Being a farmer is an addiction; even when I've done other things, I haven't been able to stay away from it for very long.

How I harvest: I get up between 7:30 and 8 o'clock every morning. In the spring, you're preparing the land, pruning the raspberries and blackberries, and that keeps up until early June, when you start to harvest. At that point you're still trying to beat the weeds back, and get the berries to market.

What's special about what we do: It's all about knowing your crops and knowing how they react. It's a lot like raising children; plants are living things, and you have to protect them from diseases over wintering or they won't do as well.

My favorite way to eat it all: I eat a lot of our berries just plain. Maybe to strawberries or raspberries, I'll add just a little cream and sugar. But I also love a good blueberry pie. My wife makes truly terrific jams and preserves for our family.

Applesauce

Makes 8 ounces

Ingredients:

4 Cortland apples

4 McIntosh apples

4 cups apple cider

Directions:

Peel and core the apples.

Place them in a heavy-bottomed pot and simmer with the apple cider for 2 to 3 hours.

When the apples are soft, puree the mixture.

Return to the stove and cook until the sauce thickens. Serve hot or cold.

Lemon Crème Fraîche

Serves 6

Ingredients:

½ tablespoon shallots, chopped

1 lemon, zested

½ of 1 lemon, juiced

2 tablespoon chives, chopped fine

1 ¼ cups crème fraîche

½ cup sour cream

Salt and pepper to taste

Directions:

Combine all ingredients in a bowl until thoroughly integrated. Cover and chill until ready to use.

Tartar Sauce

Serves 8

Ingredients:

½ cup kosher dill pickles, diced small

½ cup onion, diced small

⅓ cup capers

¼ cup parsley, chopped

1½ cups mayonnaise

3 tablespoons lemon juice

2 tablespoons Thai chili garlic sauce (optional for spicy Tartar Sauce)

Directions:

Mix all ingredients together in a bowl. Cover and chill until ready to serve.

Tomato Basil Sauce

Serves 6

Ingredients:

4 tablespoons extra virgin olive oil

2 cloves fresh garlic, chopped

4 tablespoons fresh basil, chopped

1 medium onion, diced

1 cup hearty red wine

2 28-ounce cans whole tomatoes in juice

2 ounces tomato paste

Salt and pepper

Directions:

Heat the olive oil in a saucepan and add the garlic, half of the basil, and onions.

Cook the onions until transparent, add the wine, and reduce by half.

Open the tomatoes and lightly crush them by hand in the juice, then add to the pan.

Stir all ingredients together, bring to a boil, and reduce to a simmer.

Stir in the tomato paste and simmer for 30 to 45 minutes.

Remove from the heat, stir in the remaining basil, and season with salt and pepper.

Best served with freshly grated Parmesan cheese.

Bourbon BBQ Sauce

Serves 8

Ingredients:

4 cups ketchup

1 cup water

1 tablespoon garlic, chopped

½ cup brown sugar

1 teaspoon Tabasco sauce

1 tablespoon Worcestershire sauce

1 bay leaf

½ cup Jim Beam bourbon

Directions:

Combine all ingredients in a pot except for the bourbon.

Bring to a boil and cook for 1 hour.

Add bourbon, simmer for 20 more minutes.

Red Wine Sauce

Serves 6

Ingredients:

2 tablespoons shallots or red onion, chopped

1 tablespoon olive oil

2 tablespoons tomato paste

½ cup red wine

2 cups Veal or Oxtail Stock (substitute with beef stock, if necessary) (see page 164)

1 sprig fresh thyme

Directions:

Sauté the shallots or red onion in the oil until well browned.

Add in the tomato paste and cook over medium heat for 5 minutes, stirring occasionally to prevent burning.

Add in the red wine and reduce by half.

Add the stock and thyme and let slowly simmer for 30 minutes.

Remove from the heat and strain before serving.

Chicken Stock

Makes 6 cups

Ingredients:

2 pounds chicken backs, without skin or bone

¼ cup carrot, chopped

¼ cup celery, chopped

½ cup onion, chopped

2 bay leaves

1 sprig fresh thyme

12 cups water

Directions:

Place all ingredients in a stock pot. Bring to a boil and reduce to a simmer.

Skim the top of the stock to remove any grease or foam that may form.

Cook on a very slow simmer for 4 hours, skimming occasionally.

Remove from the heat and strain through a fine strainer.

Cool immediately for further use.

Ham Hock Stock

Makes 4 to 6 cups

Ingredients:

2 pounds smoked ham hocks

¼ cup carrot, chopped

¼ cup celery, chopped

¼ cup onion, chopped

1 hot pepper

1 sprig fresh thyme

2 bay leaves

8 cups water

Directions:

Place all of the ingredients into a large saucepan and bring to a boil.

Reduce heat to a simmer, cover, and cook 6 to 8 hours.

Remove from the heat and strain through a fine strainer.

Cool immediately for further use.

Veal or Oxtail Stock

Makes 4 to 6 cups

Ingredients:

2 pounds veal bones or oxtails

2 tablespoons olive oil

¼ cup carrot, chopped

¼ cup celery, chopped

½ cup onion, chopped

2 tablespoons tomato paste

1 bay leaf

1 sprig fresh thyme

8 cups water

Directions:

In a heavy bottomed saucepan, brown the veal bones or oxtails well in the oil.

Remove the veal bones or oxtails and add the carrot, celery, and onion and brown.

Add the tomato paste and cook for 5 minutes.

Place the veal bones or oxtails back into the pan. Add the bay leaf and thyme and cover with the water.

Bring the stock to a boil and stir well to remove any food that may be stuck on the bottom of the pan.

Reduce heat to a very slow simmer and cook covered for 6 to 8 hours.

Remove from the heat and strain the stock through a fine strainer.

Cool immediately for further use.

Dry Brine

Makes 1 batch

Ingredients:

1 pound kosher salt

⅓ pound white pepper

1 cup sugar

Directions:

Mix all ingredients together well and store in a plastic container.

Wet Brine

Makes 1 batch

Ingredients:

1 gallon water

1 cup kosher salt

¼ cup brown sugar

1 dash cayenne pepper

1 tablespoon black peppercorns

2 bay leaves

1 sprig fresh thyme

1 head garlic, cut in half

4 cloves

Directions:

Place all ingredients together in a medium saucepan. Over high heat, bring the mixture to a boil. Reduce heat to low and simmer for 15 minutes.

Allow to cool before serving. Keep covered and chilled until ready to use.

Maple Wet Brine

Makes 1 batch

Ingredients:

1 cup Grade B or extra dark maple syrup

4 cups Wet Brine (see above)

Directions:

Mix all ingredients together and keep covered and chilled until ready to use.

Dry BBQ Rub

Makes 1 batch

Ingredients:

2 tablespoons paprika

2 tablespoons chili powder

2 teaspoons salt

2 teaspoons onion powder

2 teaspoons garlic powder

2 teaspoons cumin powder

1 teaspoon cayenne

1 teaspoon dried thyme

1 teaspoon white pepper

Directions:

Mix all ingredients together in a bowl. Keep covered until ready to use.

Pastrami Rub

Makes 1 batch

Ingredients:

1 cup pink peppercorns

½ cup black peppercorns

½ cup coriander seed

½ cup ground ginger powder

Directions:

In a coffee mill, coarsely grind the peppercorns with the coriander seed. Mix with the ginger powder.

Store covered until ready to use.

Maple BBQ Rub

Makes 1 batch

Ingredients:

4 cups maple sugar

½ cup thyme

3 cups paprika

1½ cups cumin

2 cups garlic powder

1 cup onion powder

½ cup mustard powder

¼ cup cayenne

1 cup celery salt

Directions:

Mix all ingredients together in a bowl. Cover and chill until ready to serve.

Chicken Herbs

Makes 1 batch

Ingredients:

6 tablespoons fresh parsley, chopped

3 tablespoons fresh chives, chopped

3 tablespoons fresh thyme, chopped

3 tablespoons fresh marjoram, chopped

3 tablespoons fresh tarragon, chopped

3 tablespoons fresh rosemary, chopped

1¼ tablespoons fresh sage, chopped

Directions:

Chop all herbs separately, and very fine. Combine in a medium-sized bowl and mix thoroughly. Keep covered until ready to use.

Chicken Mustard

Makes 2 cups

Ingredients:

1 cup whole-grain mustard

½ cup Dijon mustard

4 tablespoons horseradish

4 tablespoons maple syrup

Directions:

Add all ingredients to a medium-sized bowl and mix together thoroughly. Keep covered and refrigerated until ready to use.

Maple-Stout Marinade

Makes 8 cups

Ingredients:

12 tablespoons Dijon mustard

1 cup maple syrup

4 cups stout

1 cup red wine vinegar

4 tablespoons Worcestershire sauce

8 bay leaves

4 teaspoons Tabasco sauce

2 cups onion, finely diced

Directions:

In a medium saucepan, mix the mustard and maple syrup together. Add the remaining ingredients and bring to a boil over high heat. Reduce heat and let simmer for 2 to 3 minutes.

Let cool before using.

Chicken Demi-glace

Makes about 3 cups

Ingredients:

1 pound chicken bones

¼ cup carrot, chopped

¼ cup celery, chopped

¼ cup onion, chopped

½ cup red wine

2 tablespoons tomato paste

6 cups Chicken Stock
(see page 163)

2 bay leaves

Directions:

Preheat oven to 350 degrees.

Place the chicken bones on a cookie sheet and in the oven to brown (about 45 minutes).

Remove from the oven and drain any fat, do not discard fat.

In a heavy bottomed saucepan, brown the carrot, celery, and onion in 2 tablespoons of the chicken fat.

Add the red wine and reduce by half.

Place the remaining ingredients into the pan with the browned bones.

Bring the sauce to a boil and reduce to a simmer.

Reduce the sauce by half.

Remove from the heat and strain through a fine strainer and cool immediately.

Maple-Soy Marinade

Serves 10

Ingredients:

1 cup maple syrup

1 cup soy sauce

1 cup safflower oil

1 cup cider vinegar

1 cup lime juice

4 cloves garlic, chopped

Directions:

Mix all ingredients together in a bowl. Cover and chill until ready to use.

Verrill Farm, Concord, Massachusetts

Name: Steve Verrill

What I make: We produce healthful food of superb flavor, primarily vegetables and strawberries.

How I got started: After struggling economically as a dairy farmer for many years, in 1990 we switched our emphasis to produce. We began with pick-your-own and farmers' markets. After that we made some restaurant contacts and started delivering to a few restaurants, including Henrietta's Table. In 1994 we constructed a farmstand, to which we added a large kitchen in 2000.

What I do on a typical day: My schedule varies with the seasons. In winter, I give a lot of input into seed selection. In spring, I do a lot of plowing in preparation for planting the crops. As we get into corn season, I go out with the crew, picking corn every morning at 6. As the season for crops ends, I take special effort to get cover crops planted in a timely manner. All through the year, I fill in on all the jobs on the farm as needed, including a lot of maintenance and repair, problem solving, and managing and motivating employees in different aspects of the business. I consider myself a professional generalist, which helps make life fun and interesting.

What's special about what we do: Our emphasis is on flavor and quality. We take great pains in everything from seed selection to harvesting at the optimum time, and follow through with prompt cleaning, cooling, and packing.

My favorite way to eat it all: In recent years, I've become fond of roasted root vegetables. As for sweet corn, I enjoy eating it raw in the field as we pick it each morning. If it doesn't taste good raw, it's difficult to turn it into a tasty dish on the table. When we cook corn, I like a maximum of three minutes in boiling water. Tomatoes are great fun with all the different varieties we grow (about 75 varieties), so each person can find their own favorite colors and flavors.

Honey-Molasses Marinade

Makes 1 batch

Ingredients:

2½ cups Dijon mustard

2 cups honey

2 cups molasses

60 ounces porter beer

3 cups red wine vinegar

8 tablespoons Worcestershire sauce

10 bay leaves

8 teaspoons Tabasco sauce

4 cups onion, diced

Directions:

In a medium saucepan over high heat, combine all ingredients and bring to a boil. Let cool and cover. Keep chilled until ready to use.

Mushroom Marinade

Makes 1 batch

Ingredients:

1¼ cups safflower oil

½ cup rice wine vinegar

2½ tablespoons shallots, chopped

Salt and pepper to taste

Directions:

Combine all ingredients in a bowl and whisk together.

Season with salt and pepper to taste.

Garlic and Cumin Dressing

Serves 8

Ingredients:

8 cloves garlic

A dash of olive oil

⅓ cup balsamic vinegar

⅓ cup red wine vinegar

1¼ cups olive oil

2 teaspoons cilantro, chopped

2 teaspoons thyme, chopped

1¼ teaspoons sage, chopped

2 teaspoons basil, chopped

½ teaspoon cumin

4 tablespoons honey

Directions:

Preheat oven to 350 degrees.

Place the garlic cloves in a casserole pan with a dash of olive oil. Place in the oven for 15 to 20 minutes, or until golden brown.

Puree garlic in a food processor.

Transfer 3½ teaspoons of the garlic puree to a medium-sized bowl. Add all remaining ingredients and whisk together.

Citrus Vinaigrette

Serves 8 to 10

Ingredients:

1 bunch chives, chopped

⅛ cup tarragon, chopped

¾ cup orange juice

¼ cup lime juice

¼ cup lemon juice

3 cups safflower oil

Directions:

Combine all ingredients in a bowl.

Creamy Peppercorn Dressing

Serves 6

Ingredients:

½ cup sour cream

¾ cup mayonnaise

¾ cup buttermilk

2½ teaspoons apple cider vinegar

⅛ cup cracked black pepper

⅓ teaspoon salt

Directions:

Mix all ingredients together in a bowl. Cover and chill until ready to serve.

Blue Cheese Vinaigrette

Serves 6

Ingredients:

½ cup blue cheese, crumbled

1¼ cups olive oil

4 tablespoons red wine vinegar

2½ tablespoons lemon juice

Salt and pepper to taste

Directions:

Combine all ingredients in a bowl. Season with salt and pepper to taste.

Creamy Garlic Dressing

Serves 8

Ingredients:

1½ cups mayonnaise

2 tablespoons Dijon mustard

2 anchovies, very finely minced

2 tablespoons lemon juice

2 teaspoons sherry vinegar

2 teaspoons cracked black pepper

4 tablespoons Parmesan cheese, grated

½ teaspoon garlic, finely chopped

Directions:

Into a medium-sized bowl, add the mayonnaise, mustard, and anchovies together. Mix together with an electric mixer to thoroughly combine.

While the mixer is on low speed, slowly add the lemon juice and sherry vinegar to the mixture until completely incorporated.

Add the cracked black pepper, Parmesan cheese, and garlic. Chill until ready to serve.

Warm Bacon Vinaigrette

Serves 8

Ingredients:

½ cup smoked bacon, diced small

½ cup Spanish onions, diced small

⅓ tablespoon garlic, chopped

2½ tablespoons honey

¼ cup Dijon mustard

1¼ cups olive oil

¼ cup Champagne vinegar

Salt and pepper to taste

Directions:

In a medium frying pan, cook bacon until crispy. Add onion and garlic and continue cooking until they are transparent.

Place bacon mix in a medium-sized bowl with honey and mustard.

Whisk in oil and vinegar and season to taste. Chill.

Warm over low heat on the stove just before serving.

Walnut Vinaigrette

Serves 8

Ingredients:

1¼ cups walnuts

⅜ cup walnut oil

1⅝ cups safflower oil

⅝ cup rice wine vinegar

3 tablespoons chives, chopped

Salt and pepper to taste

Directions:

Preheat oven to 350 degrees.

Toast walnuts in the oven for 5 to 7 minutes or until golden brown. Once cooled, crush them by hand with a knife until they are the size of small peas.

Combine oils, vinegar, and chives in a medium-sized bowl and whisk together.

Season with salt and pepper and add crushed walnuts.

Mustard Vinaigrette

Serves 10

Ingredients:

2 cups safflower oil

⅓ cup Dijon mustard

¼ cup grainy mustard

½ cup cider vinegar

4 tablespoons shallots, minced

Salt and pepper to taste

Directions:

Whisk all ingredients together and season with salt and pepper.

Champagne-Lemon Herb Vinaigrette

Serves 8

Ingredients:

1¼ tablespoons shallots, chopped

1 tablespoon garlic, chopped

2½ tablespoons fresh lemon juice

1 lemon

2 tablespoons Dijon mustard

1¼ tablespoons honey

1 cup safflower oil

2½ tablespoons Champagne vinegar

2 tablespoons fresh thyme, stems removed and chopped

2 tablespoons fresh tarragon, stems removed and chopped

2 tablespoons fresh Italian parsley, stems removed and chopped

Salt and pepper to taste

Directions:

Combine first 6 ingredients in a blender and mix.

Slowly add in oils and the vinegar on high speed. Add herbs and salt and pepper.

Herb Vinaigrette

Serves 8

Feel free to substitute the red wine vinegar in this recipe with lemon juice.

Ingredients:

⅓ cup red wine vinegar

1 cup safflower oil

1½ tablespoons basil, chopped

1½ tablespoons fresh cilantro, chopped

2 tablespoons fresh parsley, chopped

1½ tablespoons fresh tarragon, chopped

1½ tablespoons fresh thyme, chopped

1½ tablespoons fresh sage, chopped

1 cup shallots, chopped

Salt and pepper to taste

Directions:

Combine all ingredients in a medium-sized bowl and whisk together. Season with salt and pepper.

Creamy Blue Cheese Dressing

Serves 10

Ingredients:

2 cups sour cream or crème fraîche

1 pint buttermilk

⅛ cup lemon juice

12 ounces blue cheese

Salt and pepper to taste

Directions:

Combine the first 3 ingredients and crumble blue cheese into the mixture. Season with salt and pepper to taste.

Maple~Pecan Vinaigrette

Serves 6

Ingredients:

¾ cup pecans

⅓ cup rice wine vinegar

5 tablespoons maple syrup

1½ cups safflower oil

Salt and pepper to taste

Directions:

Preheat oven or toaster oven to 350 degrees.

Spread pecans on an oiled cookie sheet and toast evenly for approximately 10 minutes.

Combine all ingredients. Keep chilled until ready to use.

Basil Dressing

Serves 8

Ingredients:

10 tablespoons fresh basil, chopped

5 tablespoons fresh curly parsley, chopped

1 cup sour cream

1 cup mayonnaise

¼ cup buttermilk

⅛ cup cider vinegar

½ teaspoon garlic, chopped

½ teaspoon capers

Salt and pepper to taste

Directions:

Wash and chop the herbs to a rough texture.

Mix all ingredients in a blender. Season with salt and pepper.

Blood Orange Vinaigrette

Serves 10

*If you don't have blood orange juice available, feel
free to substitute fresh regular orange juice.*

Ingredients:

2 cups blood orange juice

1 cup safflower oil

2 tablespoons fresh tarragon, chopped

2 shallots, minced

4 blood oranges, peeled and sectioned

Salt and pepper to taste

Directions:

In a medium-sized bowl, mix all ingredients together thoroughly. Cover and chill until ready to serve.

Desserts & Drinks

Pig Gingersnap Cookies

Any sweets connoisseur knows that just because something comes last, doesn't mean it isn't the best (often just the opposite). That belief is mixed into the creation of every dessert we serve at Henrietta's Table, and just as with all of the other dishes that precede that final course, we do everything we can to highlight the pure ingredients—many of which are based on fruits that are straight from the orchards, sharp-flavored spices, and deeply creamy puddings.

Of course, as with the drinks in this same chapter, each dessert here tastes its very best when made and served in its season. The pie recipe that follows, for example, is adaptable to almost any kind of filling you want to use, and while the filling recipes we include are always a big hit at the restaurant, we encourage you to use whatever happen to be the freshest and most seasonal flavors you can get your hands on. That's the making of a very sweet ending indeed.

Baked Stuffed Apple

Serves 4 to 6

This recipe uses homemade puff pastry; if you opt to use store-bought, go ahead and skip to the steps for making the filling. However you prepare it, this dessert is particularly delicious served with vanilla or cinnamon-flavored ice cream.

Ingredients:

For the pastry (yields enough dough for about 6 to 8 apples):

1½ cups all-purpose flour

2 ounces butter, cut in larger, ½-ounce sizes

½ pound butter, cut into pea-sized cubes

1 teaspoon salt

½ cup cold water

For the stuffed apple filling:

1 cup all-purpose flour

3 ounces butter, chilled

¼ cup dark brown sugar

½ cup light brown sugar

⅛ teaspoon salt

½ cup assorted diced dried fruit (cranberries, cherries, apricots, and/or raisins)

1 ounce rum

4 to 6 apples

For the apples:

Milk

Granulated sugar

Directions:

To make the pastry: Place flour in a food processor equipped with a steel blade. Add the larger pieces of butter and pulse 10 to 12 times at 1-second pulses. Then put in the small butter cubes and pulse 2 times.

Add salt to the cold water, add water to the flour mixture, and pulse until a ball just begins to form.

Cover the dough with a damp cloth and place in the refrigerator overnight. Take out and roll out on a cold marble surface so butter doesn't melt. Roll it into a 6x12-inch rectangle. Fold into thirds along the short side. Roll back out into a rectangle about a ¼-inch thick, then roll it up the long way, like a jelly roll. Let rest at least 2 hours or overnight.

Flatten the jelly-roll shaped dough and roll out to ⅛-inch thick, then cut with a pizza cutter into 4x4-inch squares.

Save the scraps to make decorative leaves to garnish the baked stuffed apple once it has been wrapped.

Preheat oven to 375 degrees.

To make the filling:

Blend the flour and butter in mixer with a paddle until it reaches a sand-like texture.

Add the brown sugar and salt to the mixture. Blend to incorporate and add dried fruits and rum. Mix to a paste-like texture.

To make the apples:
Peel and core the apples. Once cored, hollow them out a little wider using a small knife, and reserve the apple that results from the additional coring.

Take some of the extra apple that results from widening the center and stuff it into the bottom of the apples to minimize any leakage during baking.

Stuff the apples with the filling using a spoon, then take the stuffed apples and place them on top of the precut puff pastry squares, and fold the corners of the puff pastry up to the top of the apple. Brush the outside of pastry with some milk and sprinkle lightly with granulated sugar.

Using some of the puff pastry scraps, cut out the shape of several leaves with a paring knife and mark in some veins. Place 1 on top of each apple. Let rest in refrigerator for about 30 minutes or overnight.

Bake apples in preheated oven. Turn oven down to 350 degrees and bake until apple is soft when poked with a toothpick and puff pastry is a deep golden brown.

Let rest out of the oven for 10 to 20 minutes before serving.

Fresh Pumpkin Whoopie Pies

Makes 12 individual pies

Ingredients:

1¼ cups sugar

½ cup oil

3 eggs

2 cups all-purpose flour

1½ teaspoons baking soda

¼ teaspoon salt

½ teaspoon cinnamon

¼ teaspoon ground cloves

½ teaspoon nutmeg

¼ teaspoon baking powder

1 cup fresh pumpkin puree

½ pint heavy cream

½ tablespoon confectioners' sugar

¼ teaspoon cinnamon, freshly grated if possible

Directions:

Preheat oven to 325 degrees.

Mix sugar and oil together in a medium-sized bowl, until blended thoroughly. Break and add in eggs slowly.

Sift flour, baking soda, salt, cinnamon, cloves, nutmeg, and baking powder together into a medium-sized bowl. Mix into sugar-and-eggs mixture. Incorporate pumpkin puree.

Put in refrigerator to set, about 1 hour. Use a medium-sized ice cream scoop to create 12 balls approximately twice the size of a marble, place on a sheet pan, and press a bit with hands to give a rounder shape.

Bake for about 12 minutes, or until a toothpick comes out clean.

Whip cream to stiff peaks, adding sugar and cinnamon while whipping.

Add a medium-sized dollop of the cream between 2 pumpkin cakes, creating a sandwich. Sprinkle with confectioners' sugar or leave as-is to serve.

Hasty Indian Pudding

Makes 6 to 8

This pudding recipe, brought over from England, was originally made using a sweetened porridge of flour, tapioca or oatmeal, and milk. When it was made in Colonial America, it became known as Indian Pudding, because it was adapted to use cornmeal—an ingredient much cheaper and more readily available. We serve it warm with some fresh cream and a drizzle of maple syrup.

Ingredients:

4 cups light cream

¼ cup molasses

⅓ cup light brown sugar

6 tablespoons cornmeal

2 eggs

2 egg yolks

1 teaspoon cinnamon

1 teaspoon ginger

⅛ teaspoon nutmeg

¼ cup butter, cut into medium-sized pieces

Fresh cream, whipped

Maple syrup

Directions:

Place the cream in a saucepan and bring to a boil.

Add the molasses and brown sugar, and bring to a simmer.

In a medium-sized bowl, stir cornmeal into eggs and yolks, followed by spices.

Once cream and molasses mixture has come to a simmer, add one-quarter of the mixture slowly to the egg mixture while whisking.

Slowly whisk the egg mixture back into the remaining cream mixture over low heat until it reaches another simmer. Remove from the stove and add in the butter, stirring to incorporate.

Serve warm with fresh whipped cream and maple syrup.

Pumpkin Bread

Yields 2 loaves

Ingredients:

3 cups sugar

1⅛ cups oil

5 eggs

4 cups all-purpose flour

1 tablespoon baking soda

¼ teaspoon salt

1 teaspoon cinnamon

½ teaspoon nutmeg

¾ teaspoon baking powder

2¼ cups pumpkin puree

Directions:

Preheat oven to 350 degrees.

Grease 2 loaf pans.

Vigorously mix sugar and oil. Add eggs slowly while mixing.

In a separate bowl, sift together flour, baking soda, salt, cinnamon, nutmeg, and baking powder. Add to the sugar-and-eggs mixture.

Add in the pumpkin puree, and mix thoroughly.

Divide batter into the pans.

Bake for approximately 30 minutes or until an inserted toothpick comes out clean.

Gingerbread Cake and Fresh Cream

Serves 8 to 10

Ingredients:

10 ounces butter

1¼ cups molasses

⅔ cup hot water

1¼ cup sugar

4½ cups all-purpose flour

1¾ teaspoon baking soda

2 teaspoons cinnamon

¼ teaspoon nutmeg

2 tablespoons ginger

2 eggs, beaten

1 tablespoon crème fraîche

1 tablespoon crystallized ginger, finely diced

Directions:

Preheat oven to 325 degrees.

Grease the bottom of a 10-inch cake pan.

In a medium saucepan, melt butter on the stove and add in the molasses and hot water. Bring mixture to a simmer.

Sift all of the dry ingredients into a large bowl. Add in the simmering molasses mixture and incorporate fully.

Add eggs and crème fraîche.

Pour into the pre-greased pan and bake for approximately 40 minutes, or until a toothpick inserted into the middle of the cake comes out clean.

Cool the cake for at least 20 minutes, slice, and serve warm with a dollop of fresh whipped cream. Sprinkle with the crystallized ginger as a garnish.

Vanilla Cheesecake
and Native Fresh Berry Compote

Serves 8 to 10

Ingredients:

1½ cups graham cracker crumbs

⅛ cup butter, melted

3¼ cups cream cheese, softened

1 cup sugar

5 eggs

1 teaspoon vanilla extract

½ cup sour cream

½ cup heavy cream

4 cups mixed berries (raspberries, quartered strawberries, blueberries, blackberries)

¼ cup sugar

Directions:

Preheat oven to 350 degrees.

Mix graham cracker crumbs and butter, and press into bottom of a 10-inch springform cake pan.

Bake for 5 minutes or so until toasted and golden brown. Let cool.

Mix cream cheese and sugar until no lumps remain and sugar has dissolved. In a separate bowl, mix the eggs and vanilla. Slowly add the egg mixture to the cream cheese mixture, then add the sour cream, then the heavy cream.

Fill a large casserole dish (large enough to fit the cake pan in) one-quarter full with water.

Pour the batter into the cake pan holding the graham cracker crust and place the pan into the larger casserole dish with the water. Bake in oven for about 1 hour until light brown in color. Tap the cake pan with a spoon while in oven—when ready, the cake should jiggle like a bowl of Jell-O. Let cool, and chill overnight in the refrigerator.

Mix 1 cup of the berry mixture with the sugar, and simmer in a small saucepan on low heat. Puree the mixture in a blender (or leave chunky if you prefer) and add the remaining berries.

Remove cake from the springform pan and cut with a hot knife.

Serve topped with a spoon of berry compote.

Winter Berry Pudding

Serves 4 to 6

Ingredients:

1 teaspoon plain gelatin powder

4 teaspoons cold water

½ pint raspberries

½ pint blueberries

½ pint blackberries

1 pint strawberries

1 loaf of good soft white bread

Directions:

Soften the gelatin in cold water.

Place all of the berries in a saucepan and slowly heat until just before a boil. Remove from the heat, and add the gelatin mixture. Cool the berry mix.

Cut the crust off the bread and roll each slice flat with a rolling pin.

Dip the bread into the berry mix to moisten slightly.

In a mold, overlap the slices to completely cover the mold. In the center, add the berry mix to fill the mold. Cool for at least 4 hours or overnight.

Invert the mold onto a plate to be served.

Pig Gingersnap Cookies

Makes about 2 dozen

At the restaurant, we serve these gingery treats at the very end of the meal when we present the check—and we call them pig cookies because we cut them into the shape of a pig, in honor of Henrietta. But of course, they are just as delicious cut into any shape you prefer.

Ingredients:

2 sticks butter, very soft

1¼ cups sugar

⅓ cup molasses

1 large egg

2½ teaspoons cinnamon

2⅛ tablespoons ground ginger

2 teaspoons baking soda

2 cups all-purpose flour

Directions:

Vigorously blend the butter and sugar in a bowl with a whisk or fork, until the sugar is dissolved.

Fold in the molasses, then whisk in the egg.

Sift together the spices, baking soda, and flour. Then stir into the butter mixture until blended.

Wrap tightly and chill for at least 2 hours.

Preheat oven to 350 degrees.

Roll the dough out to ⅛-inch thick and cut cookies out in desired shapes. Place onto a baking sheet.

Bake 8 to 12 minutes or until golden brown. Let cool and serve.

Farmer's Custard

Serves 6

Ingredients:

½ tablespoon gelatin

2 cups heavy cream

½ cup powdered sugar

½ cup plain yogurt

½ cup buttermilk

Directions:

Soften gelatin in 1 cup of the cream.

Heat remaining cream and sugar over low heat. Add gelatin to dissolve.

Remove from heat and stir in yogurt and buttermilk. Pour into 6 large ramekins. Chill overnight, then serve.

Anadama Bread

Serves 8 to 10

It's a bit of New England lore how this scrumptious dessert got its name. History has it that a Colonial farmer's wife, "Ana," accidentally put too much flour in the corn bread, causing the farmer to scream, "Ana, damn her!"

Ingredients:

1 cup water

1 tablespoon butter

¼ teaspoon salt

¼ cup cornmeal

⅓ cup molasses

⅓ ounce fresh yeast

½ cup cold water

4 cups high-gluten bread flour

Directions:

Boil the first amount of water, then add the butter and salt.

Add the cornmeal and cook until the mixture has thickened. After a couple of minutes, add the molasses.

In a separate bowl, combine the fresh yeast and cold water and set aside.

Pour the hot molasses mixture into a medium-sized mixing bowl. Blend in a mixer with a paddle on medium speed until cooled to room temperature.

Once cooled, replace paddle with a dough hook and add the fresh yeast and water mixture, followed by the flour. Mix for 8 minutes on medium speed. Set in bowl and allow to rise in refrigerator overnight.

Pull the dough from refrigerator and let it sit at room temperature for about 1 hour. Punch dough down and form into a loaf shape.

Allow loaf to proof in a warm place for about 1 hour until it has doubled in size.

Preheat oven to 350 degrees.

Bake for about 25 minutes to a golden brown. Let come to room temperature before serving.

H.T. Daily Pie

Serves 8 to 10

Everyday, our kitchen remakes this flaky, buttery little masterpiece based on what fillings are freshest. I urge you to do the same, using whatever fruit-, nut- or chocolate-based center appeals most (though several of our favorite fillings can be found on the following pages). No matter what filling you use, the results are almost always addictive.

Ingredients:

For pie shell:

2¼ cups pastry flour

1 pound butter, chilled and diced

About ½ cup water

3 teaspoons sugar

½ teaspoon salt

For crumb topping:

2¼ cups all-purpose flour

½ pound butter, chilled and diced

¾ cup dark brown sugar

1¼ cups light brown sugar

½ teaspoon salt

Directions:

To make the pie shell:

Mix the flour with the butter until it reaches a sandy texture.

In a bowl, combine water, sugar, and salt until dissolved.

Add three-quarters of the water to the above mixture. Once dough comes together, add the rest of the water to the bowl and blend. Chill for about 2 hours or overnight.

Preheat oven to 350 degrees.

Roll out dough to ¼-inch thick and cut rounds.

Form the pie shell into a pie tin and form a rimmed edge.

Line the shell with a coffee filter or a piece of wax paper, then fill the lining with beans, rice, or pennies. Bake that way until the crust rims are golden brown, about 15 minutes.

Remove from the oven, and remove lining and filler. Cool. (If you're using a cold filling such as custard or cream, return the empty pie shell to the oven until whole pie shell is a deep, golden brown.)

Once cool, fill with desired filling.

To make the crumb topping:

Rub flour and cold diced butter together until they reach a sandy texture. Add brown sugar and salt to the mixture, but don't overmix. This topping should not come together; it should remain very sandy throughout the process.

Place topping evenly over the pie and return to a 350-degree oven until filling is bubbling and topping is golden brown.

Apple Pie Filling

Serves 8 to 10

Ingredients:

2 ounces butter

1 pound apples (or 8 to 10 apples), peeled, cored, and cut into chunks

⅓ cup granulated sugar

¼ cup light brown sugar

⅔ teaspoon salt

2 tablespoons flour

½ teaspoon cinnamon

Directions:

Cook butter on stovetop in a saucepan, until it just reaches a light brown color. Be careful to remove from heat before it burns.

Fold all ingredients together in a bowl and let sit for approximately 20 to 40 minutes in a warm area, stirring every few minutes until sugar has dissolved.

Preheat oven to 350 degrees.

Fill pie bottom with mixture and top with crumb topping (see page 197). Bake for 30 minutes.

Pumpkin Pie Filling

Serves 8 to 10

Ingredients:

3½ cups pumpkin pulp, pureed

¼ cup all-purpose flour

1½ teaspoons cinnamon

¼ teaspoon nutmeg

¼ teaspoon ginger

¼ teaspoon cloves

⅛ ounce salt

1¼ packed cups light brown sugar

¼ cup corn syrup

2½ cups sweetened condensed milk

6 eggs

3¾ cup light cream

Directions:

Combine all ingredients, except eggs and cream, in a medium-sized bowl. Whisk together.

Whisk in eggs 1 at a time, followed by the cream.

Let the mixture rest overnight.

Preheat oven to 350 degrees.

Pour filling into a partially-baked 9-inch pie shell and bake about 45 minutes, until set.

Pecan Pie Filling

Serves 8 to 10

Ingredients:

2 ounces butter

¾ cup light brown sugar

2 cups light corn syrup

1 tablespoon molasses

1 tablespoon maple syrup

½ teaspoon vanilla

2 teaspoons bourbon or dark rum

6 eggs

1 cup pecan halves, lightly toasted

Directions:

Preheat oven to 350 degrees.

Cook butter on stovetop in a saucepan, until it just reaches a light brown color. Be careful to remove from heat before it burns.

Combine all ingredients except pecans and eggs in a medium-sized bowl and whisk to combine.

Then whisk in the eggs.

Place pecans on bottom of pie shell and pour the mix over top. Bake for approximately 45 minutes, or until set.

Henrietta's Table Chocolate Bread Pudding with Cognac Caramelized Bananas

Serves 10

This is a Henrietta's Table specialty that has built a cult following over the years. It's unbelievably simple, but utterly decadent.

Ingredients:

For the bread pudding:

5-7, depending on size, week-old plain croissants

4 cups heavy cream

1 cup sugar

⅓ cup Dutch processed cocoa powder

1 tablespoon vanilla

3 egg yolks

7 whole eggs

¾ cup chocolate chips

For the sauce:

1 cup heavy cream

2 cups light brown sugar

¼ cup water

½ teaspoon fresh lemon juice

2 ounces salted butter, softened

3 tablespoons cognac

3 bananas, sliced ¼-inch thick

Vanilla ice cream

Directions:

To make the bread pudding:

Preheat oven to 350 degrees.

Cut the croissants into cubes the size of a large crouton and place into a lightly greased 10-inch cake pan.

In a medium-sized saucepan, add cream, sugar, cocoa, and vanilla and bring close to a simmer while whisking to dissolve cocoa and sugar. Allow to cool slightly, then whisk in eggs and yolks.

Pour the mixture over croissants. Set aside for about 15 minutes to allow ingredients to soak into croissants. Give a final stir and then top with chocolate chips.

Fill a large pan halfway with water. Fit the cake pan inside, so it is surrounded by water.

Place both pans in the oven and bake, checking after 1 hour. If surface does not spring back, continue baking. With a small knife, make a small slice in center to ensure that there is no more liquid and that the pudding is completely cooked.

To make the sauce:

Warm cream on stovetop and whisk in brown sugar. Add water and lemon juice and let simmer for about 5 minutes.

Stir in butter and cognac and gently stir in bananas.

Spoon a healthy amount of sauce on top of each portion of warm bread pudding. Serve with vanilla ice cream.

Sangria

Serves 10

Ingredients:

½ cup strawberries

½ cup raspberries

½ cup blueberries

½ cup blackberries

¼ cup sugar

½ cup light rum

2 bottles light white wine

¼ cup orange juice

¼ cup cranberry juice

¼ cup cassis

1 cup sparkling wine

Directions:

Cover the berries with the sugar and let sit for 1 hour. Cover with the remaining ingredients and store chilled overnight.

Serve in wine glasses over ice.

Mixed Berry Smoothie

Serves 4

Ingredients:

2 ripe bananas

24 ounces fat-free plain yogurt

1 cup fresh orange juice

4 cups ice cubes

2 cups mixed berries (can be fresh or frozen)

4 tablespoons honey

Directions:

Peel the bananas and cut into slices.

Place all ingredients into a blender and blend until smooth.

Refrigerate or serve immediately.

Raspberry Lemonade

Serves 6

Ingredients:

2 cups sugar

1 pint water

1 gallon water

4 pints fresh raspberries

1 quart fresh lemon juice

Directions:

Bring the sugar and the pint of water to a boil to dissolve the sugar.

Remove from the heat to cool completely.

Combine the raspberries with the remaining water, then add the lemon juice and sugar mixture.

Chill and serve over ice.

Mulled Cider

Serves 6

Ingredients:

1 gallon fresh apple cider

2 oranges, cut in half

4 cloves

1 cinnamon stick

2 pieces star anise

4 pieces allspice

Directions:

Put all ingredients in a pot and warm over very low heat for 1 hour.

Serve hot.

Minted Iced Tea

Serves 6

Ingredients:

1 quart water

4 bags English breakfast tea

4 sprigs fresh mint

Sugar to taste

Directions:

Place the water, tea bags, and mint in a 1-quart glass jar and place in the sun for 6 hours.

Strain out the tea bags and mint, and chill for at least 1 hour.

Serve over ice with sugar.

Pop's Bloody Mary Mix

Serves 8 to 10

*This one's for my father—a recipe that changed many a Christmas morning.
It's a classic that can be served with or without alcohol—I recommend with.
I suggest 1½-2 ounces of vodka per drink.*

Ingredients:

3 dashes Tabasco sauce

3 dashes Worcestershire sauce

3 teaspoons white vinegar

Juice of ½ of 1 lemon

1 tablespoon horseradish

1 tablespoon celery seed

10 cups tomato juice

Salt and cracked black pepper to taste

10 celery sticks

Directions:

Mix ingredients together in a large pitcher.

Chill for 1 hour, and serve in individual glasses garnished with 1 celery stick each.

Index

A
Anadama Bread, 196
Anchovies
    Creamy Garlic Dressing, 172
Angelini Farming Trust, 159
Apple(s)
    Apple Chutney, 156
    Apple Pie Filling, 198
    Applesauce, 160
    Baked Stuffed Apple, 182
    Grilled Chicken Breast with Apple Cider Reduction, 131
    Mulled Cider, 205
    Pickled Apples, 150
    Roasted Spicy Apples, 152
Apple Chutney, 156
Apple Pie Filling, 198
Applesauce, 160
    Smoked and Grilled Pork Chops, 115
Apricot(s)
    Apricot and Tomato Chutney, 157
    Dried Stone Fruit Relish, 155
Apricot and Tomato Chutney, 157
Arugula
    Country Vegetable Soup, 48
    Grilled Native Asparagus, Feta, and EVOO, 78
    Pizza of Maine Rock Crab, Dulse, and Sea Salt, 100
    Roasted Beet Salad with Chèvre, Arugula, and Blood Orange
        Vinaigrette, 59
Asparagus
    Crab Cakes, 70
    Finnan Haddie, 92
    Grilled Asparagus, 136
    Grilled Citrus- and Dill-Cured Sablefish, 88
    Grilled Native Asparagus, Feta, and EVOO, 78
Au Gratin
    Blue Cheese au Gratin Potatoes, 149

B
Bacon
    Brussels Sprouts, 140
    Maple Baked Beans, 146
    Roasted Corn and Crab Chowder, 46
    Skillet Breakfast, 43
    Smoked Scallop Chowder, 50
    Venison Sausage with Smoked Bacon Sauerkraut, 110
    Warm Bacon Vinaigrette, 174
Baked Beans (see Beans)
Baked Carrots, 143
Baked Strawberry Rhubarb French Toast, 29
Baked Stuffed Apple, 182
Banana(s)
    Henrietta's Table Chocolate Bread Pudding with Cognac
        Caramelized Bananas, 201
    Mixed Berry Smoothie, 202

Barbecue (see BBQ)
Basil
    Basil Dressing, 178
    Farmer's Cheese Salad, 63
    Grilled Vegetables with Chèvre and Basil Oil, 31
    Tomato Basil Sauce, 161
Basil Dressing, 178
BBQ
    BBQ Grilled and Braised Lamb Shanks, 104
    Bourbon BBQ Sauce, 162
    Chipotle Spiced Pork, 116
    Dry BBQ Rub, 166
    Maple BBQ Rub, 166
    Pulled Pork, 107
BBQ Grilled and Braised Lamb Shanks, 104
Bean(s)
    Country Vegetable Soup, 48
    Flageolet Bean Salad, 152
    Ham Hock and Heirloom Bean Soup, 54
    Maple Baked Beans, 146
    Nana's Baked Beans, 147
    Succotash, 136
Beef
    Beef and Pork Chili, 119
    Creamed Chipped Beef on Buttermilk Biscuits, 41
    Maple Stout-Marinated Beef Brisket, 116
    Meatloaf, 110
    Pot Roast, 121
    Red Flannel Hash with Poached Eggs, 37
    River Rock Farm, 112, 117
    River Rock Farm Sirloin and Spinach Salad, 112
Beef and Pork Chili, 119
Beer
    Beef and Pork Chili, 119
    Chipotle Spiced Pork, 116
    Honey-Molasses Marinade, 170
    Maple-Stout Marinade, 167
    Maple Stout-Marinated Beef Brisket, 116
    Pale Ale-Braised Short Ribs, 103
Beet(s)
    Red Flannel Hash with Poached Eggs, 37
    Roasted Beets, 143
    Roasted Beet Salad with Chèvre, Arugula, and Blood Orange
        Vinaigrette, 59
Beet Greens
    Wilted Greens, 144
Berries
    Angelini Farming Trust, 159
    Mixed Berry Smoothie, 202
    Sangria, 202
    Spinach Salad with Goat Cheese and Spicy Pecans, 60
    Strawberry Rhubarb Compote, 158
    Vanilla Cheesecake and Native Fresh Berry Compote, 191
    Winter Berry Pudding, 192

Big Pig Gig, 14
Biscuits
    Buttermilk Biscuits, 149
    Creamed Chipped Beef on Buttermilk Biscuits, 41
Blackberries
    Angelini Farming Trust, 159
    Sangria, 202
    Vanilla Cheesecake and Native Fresh Berry Compote, 191
    Winter Berry Pudding, 192
Blood Orange Vinaigrette, 178
    Roasted Beet Salad with Chèvre, Arugula, and Blood Orange
        Vinaigrette, 59
Bloody Mary
    Pop's Bloody Mary Mix, 207
Blueberries
    Angelini Farming Trust, 159
    Sangria, 202
    Vanilla Cheesecake and Native Fresh Berry Compote, 191
    Winter Berry Pudding, 192
Blue Cheese
    Blue Cheese au Gratin Potatoes, 149
    Blue Cheese Vinaigrette, 172
    Creamy Blue Cheese Dressing, 176
    Great Hill Blue Farm, 80
    Iceberg Lettuce with Creamy Massachusetts Blue Cheese Dressing, 56
    New England Cheese Board, 69
    River Rock Farm Sirloin and Spinach Salad, 112
    Westfield Farm, 57, 69
Blue Cheese au Gratin Potatoes, 149
Blue Cheese Vinaigrette, 172
Bluefish
    Bluefish Pâté, 67
    Hot Smoked Bluefish with Beach Plum Vinaigrette, 97
Bluefish Pâté, 67
Bourbon
    Bourbon BBQ Sauce, 162
    Pecan Pie Filling, 199
Bourbon BBQ Sauce, 162
    Chipotle Spiced Pork, 116
Bread(s)
    Anadama Bread, 196
    Baked Strawberry Rhubarb French Toast, 29
    Cinnamon-Cranberry French Toast, 30
    Fondue, 33
    Henrietta's Table Chocolate Bread Pudding with Cognac
        Caramelized Bananas, 201
    Pumpkin Bread, 188
    Romaine Salad with Creamy Garlic Dressing, 62
    Tapenade Bread, 66
    Winter Berry Pudding, 192
Breakfast and Brunch Dishes, 29-43
    Baked Strawberry Rhubarb French Toast, 29
    Butternut Squash Pie, 41
    Cinnamon-Cranberry French Toast, 30
    Creamed Chipped Beef on Buttermilk Biscuits, 41
    Duck Hash, 32
    Fondue, 33
    Grilled Vegetables with Chèvre and Basil Oil, 31
    H.T. Granola, 35
    Poached Salmon with Cucumber Dill Crème Fraîche, 36
    Red Flannel Hash with Poached Eggs, 37
    Scotch Eggs, 38
    Skillet Breakfast, 43
    Whole Wheat Hotcakes, 30
Brie
    Grilled Portobello with Vermont Blythedale Farm Brie and Walnut
        Vinaigrette, 83
Brines
    Dry Brine, 165
    Duck Confit and Maple-Brined Breast, 130
    Maple Wet Brine, 165

    Wet Brine, 165
Brisket
    Maple Stout-Marinated Beef Brisket, 116
    Red Flannel Hash with Poached Eggs, 37
Brussels Sprouts, 140
Burgers
    Salmon Burgers, 95
Buttermilk
    Basil Dressing, 178
    Buttermilk Biscuits, 149
    Cornmeal-Crusted Monkfish Sandwich, 87
    Creamed Chipped Beef on Buttermilk Biscuits, 41
    Creamy Blue Cheese Dressing, 176
    Creamy Peppercorn Dressing, 172
    Farmer's Cheese Salad, 63
    Farmer's Custard, 195
Buttermilk Biscuits, 149
    Creamed Chipped Beef on Buttermilk Biscuits, 41
Butternut Squash
    Butternut Squash Pie, 41
    Butternut Squash Puree, 144
Butternut Squash Pie, 41
Butternut Squash Puree, 144

C
Cabbage
    Sugar Pumpkin Slaw, 150
Cakes
    Fresh Pumpkin Whoopie Pies, 184
    Gingerbread Cake and Fresh Cream, 190
    Vanilla Cheesecake and Native Fresh Berry Compote, 191
    Whole Wheat Hotcakes, 30
Caramelized Cauliflower, 142
Carrot(s)
    Baked Carrots, 143
    Chicken Noodle Soup, 46
    Country Vegetable Soup, 48
    Flageolet Bean Salad, 152
    Grilled Vegetables with Chèvre and Basil Oil, 31
    Henrietta's Table Chicken Potpie, 123
    Oven-Roasted Root Vegetables, 137
Casseroles
    Ham and Potato Casserole, 109
Cassis
    Sangria, 202
Cauliflower
    Caramelized Cauliflower, 142
    Mustard Pickles, 153
Celeriac
    Oven-Roasted Root Vegetables, 137
Celery
    Chicken Noodle Soup, 46
    Country Vegetable Soup, 48
    Flageolet Bean Salad, 152
    Grilled Chicken Salad with Walnuts and Grapes on a Bed of
        Romaine, 125
    Henrietta's Table Chicken Potpie, 123
    Pop's Bloody Mary Mix, 207
Celery Root Potatoes, 148
Champagne-Lemon Herb Vinaigrette, 175
Cheese
    Blue Cheese au Gratin Potatoes, 149
    Blue Cheese Vinaigrette, 172
    Bluefish Pâté, 67
    Creamed Onions, 141
    Creamy Blue Cheese Dressing, 176
    Creamy Garlic Dressing, 172
    Farmer's Cheese Salad, 63
    Fondue, 33
    Goat Cheese Polenta Cake, 148
    Great Hill Blue Farm, 80

Grilled Native Asparagus, Feta, and EVOO, 78
Grilled Portobello with Vermont Blythedale Farm Brie and Walnut
    Vinaigrette, 83
Grilled Vegetables with Chèvre and Basil Oil, 31
Grit Cakes with Mushrooms, 73
Ham and Potato Casserole, 109
Iceberg Lettuce with Creamy Massachusetts Blue Cheese Dressing, 56
Macaroni and Cheese, 145
New England Cheese Board, 69
River Rock Farm Sirloin and Spinach Salad, 112
Roasted Beet Salad with Chèvre, Arugula, and Blood Orange
    Vinaigrette, 59
Romaine Salad with Creamy Garlic Dressing, 62
Skillet Breakfast, 43
Spinach Salad with Goat Cheese and Spicy Pecans, 60
Vanilla Cheesecake and Native Fresh Berry Compote, 191
Westfield Farm, 57, 69

Cheesecake
Vanilla Cheesecake and Native Fresh Berry Compote, 191

Cherries
Baked Stuffed Apple, 182
Dried Stone Fruit Relish, 155
Sugar Pumpkin Slaw, 150

Cheshire Garden, 40
Chèvre (see Goat Cheese)
Chicken
Chicken 2 Ways, 128
Chicken Demi-glace, 168
Chicken Herbs, 167
Chicken Mustard, 167
Chicken Noodle Soup, 46
Chicken Stock, 163
Grilled Chicken Breast with Apple Cider Reduction, 131
Grilled Chicken Salad with Walnuts and Grapes on a
    Bed of Romaine, 125
Henrietta's Table Chicken Potpie, 123
Herb-Crusted Rotisserie Chicken, 132
Misty Knoll Farm, 124

Chicken Demi-glace, 168
Chicken 2 Ways, 128

Chicken Herbs, 167
Grilled Chicken Breast with Apple Cider Reduction, 131
Grilled Chicken Salad with Walnuts and Grapes on a Bed of
    Romaine, 125
Herb-Crusted Rotisserie Chicken, 132

Chicken Mustard, 167
Herb-Crusted Rotisserie Chicken, 132

Chicken Noodle Soup, 46
Chicken Stock, 163
Chili
Beef and Pork Chili, 119

Chipotle Spiced Pork, 116
Chipped Beef
Creamed Chipped Beef on Buttermilk Biscuits, 41

Chippen Farm, 33
Chocolate
Henrietta's Table Chocolate Bread Pudding with Cognac Caramelized
    Bananas, 201

Chowders (see Soups)
Chutneys, 156-157
Apple Chutney, 156
Apricot and Tomato Chutney, 157
Cranberry Chutney, 156

Cider
Apple Chutney, 156
Applesauce, 160
Cider-Braised Pork, 115
Grilled Chicken Breast with Apple Cider Reduction, 131
Mulled Cider, 205

Cider-Braised Pork, 115
Cinnamon-Cranberry French Toast, 30

Citrus
Citrus Vinaigrette, 171
Grilled Citrus- and Dill-Cured Sablefish, 88
Spiced Olives, 66

Clams
New England Lobster Bake, 91
Woodbury's Seafood, 96

Cod
Cod Fish Cakes, 74

Cod Fish Cakes, 74
Cognac
Henrietta's Table Chocolate Bread Pudding with Cognac Caramelized
    Bananas, 201

Collard Greens
Ham Hock and Heirloom Bean Soup, 54

Compotes
Strawberry Rhubarb Compote, 158
Vanilla Cheesecake and Native Fresh Berry Compote, 191

Condiments
Apple Chutney, 156
Apricot and Tomato Chutney, 157
Bourbon BBQ Sauce, 162
Cranberry Chutney, 156
Dried Stone Fruit Relish, 155
Lemon Crème Fraîche, 160
Mushroom Ketchup, 154
Smoked Tomato Ketchup, 155
Tartar Sauce, 160

Confit
Duck Confit and Maple-Brined Breast, 130

Cookies
Pig Gingersnap Cookies, 195

Corn
Flageolet Bean Salad, 152
New England Lobster Bake, 91
Roasted Corn and Crab Chowder, 46
Succotash, 136
Verrill Farm, 16, 169

Cornmeal
Anadama Bread, 196
Cornmeal-Crusted Monkfish Sandwich, 87
Hasty Indian Pudding, 187

Cornmeal-Crusted Monkfish Sandwich, 87
Country Vegetable Soup, 48
Crab
Crab Cakes, 70
Pizza of Maine Rock Crab, Dulse, and Sea Salt, 100
Roasted Corn and Crab Chowder, 46

Cranberries
Baked Stuffed Apple, 182
Cinnamon-Cranberry French Toast, 30
Cranberry Chutney, 156
Dried Stone Fruit Relish, 155
Sangria, 202

Cranberry Chutney, 156
Creamed Chipped Beef on Buttermilk Biscuits, 41
Creamed Onions, 141
Creamy Blue Cheese Dressing, 176
Iceberg Lettuce with Creamy Massachusetts Blue Cheese Dressing, 56

Creamy Garlic Dressing, 176
Romaine Salad with Creamy Garlic Dressing, 62

Creamy Peppercorn Dressing, 172
Sugar Pumpkin Slaw, 150

Crème Fraîche
Creamy Blue Cheese Dressing, 176
Gingerbread Cake and Fresh Cream, 190
Grilled Citrus- and Dill-Cured Sablefish, 88
Lemon Crème Fraîche, 160
Pizza of Maine Rock Crab, Dulse, and Sea Salt, 100
Poached Salmon with Cucumber Dill Crème Fraîche, 36

Croissants

Henrietta's Table Chocolate Bread Pudding with Cognac Caramelized
 Bananas, 201

Crumb Topping
 H.T. Daily Pie, 197

Crust
 H.T. Daily Pie, 197

Cucumber(s)
 Iceberg Lettuce with Creamy Massachusetts Blue Cheese Dressing, 56
 Kosher Dill Pickles, 151
 Mustard Pickles, 153
 Poached Salmon with Cucumber Dill Crème Fraîche, 36

Cumin
 Garlic and Cumin Dressing, 171

Custard
 Farmer's Custard, 195

D

Demi-glace
 Chicken 2 Ways, 128
 Chicken Demi-glace, 168

Desserts, 182-201
 Anadama Bread, 196
 Apple Pie Filling, 198
 Baked Stuffed Apple, 182
 Farmer's Custard, 195
 Fresh Pumpkin Whoopie Pies, 184
 Gingerbread Cake and Fresh Cream, 190
 Hasty Indian Pudding, 187
 Henrietta's Table Chocolate Bread Pudding with Cognac Caramelized
  Bananas, 201
 H.T. Daily Pie, 197
 Pecan Pie Filling, 199
 Pig Gingersnap Cookies, 195
 Pumpkin Bread, 188
 Pumpkin Pie Filling, 199
 Vanilla Cheesecake and Native Fresh Berry Compote, 191
 Winter Berry Pudding, 192

Dijon (see Mustard)

Dill
 Grilled Citrus- and Dill-Cured Sablefish, 88
 Kosher Dill Pickles, 151
 Poached Salmon with Cucumber Dill Crème Fraîche, 36

Dressings, 171-178
 Basil Dressing, 178
 Blood Orange Vinaigrette, 178
 Blue Cheese Vinaigrette, 172
 Champagne-Lemon Herb Vinaigrette, 175
 Citrus Vinaigrette, 171
 Creamy Blue Cheese Dressing, 176
 Creamy Garlic Dressing, 172
 Creamy Peppercorn Dressing, 172
 Garlic and Cumin Dressing, 171
 Herb Vinaigrette, 176
 Maple-Pecan Vinaigrette, 177
 Mustard Vinaigrette, 175
 Walnut Vinaigrette, 174
 Warm Bacon Vinaigrette, 174

Dried Stone Fruit Relish, 155

Drinks, 202-207
 Minted Iced Tea, 205
 Mixed Berry Smoothie, 202
 Mulled Cider, 205
 Pop's Bloody Mary Mix, 207
 Raspberry Lemonade, 204
 Sangria, 202

Dry BBQ Rub, 166
 BBQ Grilled and Braised Lamb Shanks, 104
 Pulled Pork, 107

Dry Brine, 165
 Duck Confit and Maple-Brined Breast, 130
 Homemade Smoked Salmon, 81

Duck
 Duck Confit and Maple-Brined Breast, 130
 Duck Hash, 32
 Duck Pastrami, 70
 Jurgielwicz Farm, 132

Duck Confit and Maple-Brined Breast, 130

Duck Hash, 32

Duck Pastrami, 70

Dulse
 Pizza of Maine Rock Crab, Dulse, and Sea Salt, 100
 Smoked Scallop Chowder, 50

E

Egg(s)
 Chippen Farm, 33
 Duck Hash, 32
 Red Flannel Hash with Poached Eggs, 37
 Scotch Eggs, 38
 Skillet Breakfast, 43

Eggplant
 Grilled Vegetables with Chèvre and Basil Oil, 31

Elysian Fields Farm, 109

Emmenthaler
 Fondue, 33

Eva's Garden, 75

F

Farmer's Cheese Salad, 63

Farmer's Custard, 195

Farms
 Angelini Farming Trust, 159
 Cheshire Garden, 40
 Chippen Farm, 33
 Elysian Fields Farm, 109
 Eva's Garden, 75
 The Farm School, 14
 Great Hill Blue Farm, 80
 Jurgielwicz Farm, 132
 Misty Knoll Farm, 124
 Nesenkeag Co-op Farm, 16, 51
 River Rock Farm, 112, 117
 Ted Mahoney, 91
 Verrill Farm, 16, 169
 Westfield Farm, 57, 69
 Woodbury's Seafood, 96

The Farm School, 14

Fennel
 Country Vegetable Soup, 48

Feta
 Grilled Native Asparagus, Feta, and EVOO, 78

Fiddleheads
 Grilled Striped Bass with Warm Fruit Salad and Pea Tendrils, 101

Finnan Haddie, 92

Fish
 Bluefish Pâté, 67
 Cod Fish Cakes, 74
 Cornmeal-Crusted Monkfish Sandwich, 87
 Finnan Haddie, 92
 Grilled Citrus- and Dill-Cured Sablefish, 88
 Grilled Striped Bass with Warm Fruit Salad and Pea Tendrils, 101
 Homemade Smoked Salmon, 81
 Hot Smoked Bluefish with Beach Plum Vinaigrette, 97
 Maple Thyme-Glazed Salmon, 98
 Poached Salmon Roll, 92
 Poached Salmon with Cucumber Dill Crème Fraîche, 36
 Salmon Burgers, 95
 Scrod, 98

Flageolet Bean(s)
 Flageolet Bean Salad, 152
 Grit Cakes with Mushrooms, 73

Flageolet Bean Salad, 152

Fondue, 33
French Toast
 Baked Strawberry Rhubarb French Toast, 29
 Cinnamon-Cranberry French Toast, 30
Fresh Pumpkin Whoopie Pies, 184
Fruit
 Angelini Farming Trust, 159
 Apple Chutney, 156
 Apple Pie Filling, 198
 Applesauce, 160
 Apricot and Tomato Chutney, 157
 Baked Strawberry Rhubarb French Toast, 29
 Baked Stuffed Apple, 182
 Blood Orange Vinaigrette, 178
 Cranberry Chutney, 156
 Dried Stone Fruit Relish, 155
 Grilled Striped Bass with Warm Fruit Salad and Pea Tendrils, 101
 Henrietta's Table Chocolate Bread Pudding with Cognac Caramelized Bananas, 201
 Mixed Berry Smoothie, 202
 Pickled Apples, 150
 Pumpkin Bread, 188
 Raspberry Lemonade, 204
 Roasted Spicy Apples, 152
 Sangria, 202
 Spinach Salad with Goat Cheese and Spicy Pecans, 60
 Strawberry Rhubarb Compote, 158
 Vanilla Cheesecake and Native Fresh Berry Compote, 191
 Winter Berry Pudding, 192

G
Garlic
 Creamy Garlic Dressing, 172
 Garlic and Cumin Dressing, 171
 Maple-Marinated Leg of Lamb with Rosemary- and Garlic-Herbed Potatoes, 106
 Romaine Salad with Creamy Garlic Dressing, 62
Garlic and Cumin Dressing, 171
Ginger
 Apple Chutney, 156
 Apricot and Tomato Chutney, 157
 Cranberry Chutney, 156
 Gingerbread Cake and Fresh Cream, 190
 Pickled Apples, 150
 Pig Gingersnap Cookies, 195
 Wilted Spinach, 138
Gingerbread Cake and Fresh Cream, 190
Goat Cheese
 Goat Cheese Polenta Cake, 148
 Grilled Vegetables with Chèvre and Basil Oil, 31
 Grit Cakes with Mushrooms, 73
 New England Cheese Board, 69
 Roasted Beet Salad with Chèvre, Arugula, and Blood Orange Vinaigrette, 59
 Spinach Salad with Goat Cheese and Spicy Pecans, 60
 Westfield Farm, 57, 69
Goat Cheese Polenta Cake, 148
Granola
 H.T. Granola, 35
Grape(s)
 Grilled Chicken Salad with Walnuts and Grapes on a Bed of Romaine, 125
Great Hill Blue Cheese
 Blue Cheese au Gratin Potatoes, 149
 Great Hill Blue Farm, 80
 River Rock Farm Sirloin and Spinach Salad, 112
Great Hill Blue Farm, 80
Greens
 Eva's Garden, 75
 Grilled Portobello with Vermont Blythedale Farm Brie and Walnut Vinaigrette, 83

 Ham Hock and Heirloom Bean Soup, 54
 Homemade Smoked Salmon, 81
 Nesenkeag Co-op Farm, 16, 51
 Roasted Beet Salad with Chèvre, Arugula, and Blood Orange Vinaigrette, 59
 Scotch Eggs, 38
 Wilted Greens, 144
Grilled Asparagus, 136
Grilled Chicken Breast with Apple Cider Reduction, 131
Grilled Chicken Salad with Walnuts and Grapes on a Bed of Romaine, 125
Grilled Citrus- and Dill-Cured Sablefish, 88
Grilled Native Asparagus, Feta, and EVOO, 78
Grilled Portobello with Vermont Blythedale Farm Brie and Walnut Vinaigrette, 83
Grilled Striped Bass with Warm Fruit Salad and Pea Tendrils, 101
Grilled Vegetables with Chèvre and Basil Oil, 31
Grit Cakes with Mushrooms, 73
Gruyère
 Fondue, 33

H
Haddock
 Finnan Haddie, 92
Ham
 Ham and Potato Casserole, 109
 Ham Hock and Heirloom Bean Soup, 54
 Ham Hock Stock, 164
 Pulled Pork, 107
Ham Hock and Heirloom Bean Soup, 54
Ham Hock Stock, 164
Hash
 Duck Hash, 32
 Red Flannel Hash with Poached Eggs, 37
Hasty Indian Pudding, 187
Henrietta's Table Chicken Potpie, 123
Henrietta's Table Chocolate Bread Pudding with Cognac Caramelized Bananas, 201
Henrietta's Table Mashed Potatoes, 146
Herb(s)
 Champagne-Lemon Herb Vinaigrette, 175
 Chicken Herbs, 167
 Eva's Garden, 75
 Herb-Crusted Rotisserie Chicken, 132
 Herb Vinaigrette, 176
Herb-Crusted Rotisserie Chicken, 132
Herb Vinaigrette, 176
Homemade Smoked Salmon, 81
Honey
 Apple Chutney, 156
 Champagne-Lemon Herb Vinaigrette, 175
 Garlic and Cumin Dressing, 171
 Honey-Molasses Marinade, 170
 Mixed Berry Smoothie, 202
 Mustard Pickles, 153
 Warm Bacon Vinaigrette, 174
 Whole Wheat Hotcakes, 30
Honey-Molasses Marinade, 170
Horseradish
 Chicken Mustard, 167
 Maple Thyme-Glazed Salmon, 98
 Massachusetts Oysters, Preserved Lemon Maine Vodka and Horseradish, 76
 Pop's Bloody Mary Mix, 207
Hotcakes
 Whole Wheat Hotcakes, 30
Hot Smoked Bluefish with Beach Plum Vinaigrette, 97
H.T. Daily Pie, 197
 Henrietta's Table Chicken Potpie, 123
H.T. Granola, 35

I

Iceberg Lettuce with Creamy Massachusetts Blue Cheese Dressing, 56
Indian Pudding
    Hasty Indian Pudding, 187

J

Jurgielwicz Farm, 132

K

Kale
    Wilted Greens, 144
Ketchup
    Bourbon BBQ Sauce, 162
    Mushroom Ketchup, 154
    Smoked Tomato Ketchup, 155
Kirshwasser
    Fondue, 33
Kosher Dill Pickles, 151
    Tartar Sauce, 160
Kumquat(s)
    Cranberry Chutney, 156

L

Lamb
    BBQ Grilled and Braised Lamb Shanks, 104
    Elysian Fields Farm, 109
    Maple-Marinated Leg of Lamb with Rosemary- and Garlic-Herbed Potatoes, 106
Lemon(s)
    Champagne-Lemon Herb Vinaigrette, 175
    Citrus Vinaigrette, 171
    Grilled Asparagus, 136
    Grilled Citrus- and Dill-Cured Sablefish, 88
    Grilled Native Asparagus, Feta, and EVOO, 78
    Lemon Crème Fraîche, 160
    Massachusetts Oysters, Preserved Lemon Maine Vodka and Horseradish, 76
    Preserved Lemons, 158
    Raspberry Lemonade, 204
Lemonade
    Raspberry Lemonade, 204
Lettuce
    Grilled Chicken Salad with Walnuts and Grapes on a Bed of Romaine, 125
    Iceberg Lettuce with Creamy Massachusetts Blue Cheese Dressing, 56
    Poached Salmon with Cucumber Dill Crème Fraîche, 36
    Romaine Salad with Creamy Garlic Dressing, 62
Lima Beans
    Succotash, 136
Lobster
    Lobster Chowder, 53
    New England Lobster Bake, 91
    Ted Mahoney, 91

M

Macaroni and Cheese, 145
Mahoney, Ted, 91
Maple
    Baked Carrots, 143
    Baked Strawberry Rhubarb French Toast, 29
    Butternut Squash Puree, 144
    Chicken Mustard, 167
    Cinnamon-Cranberry French Toast, 30
    Duck Confit and Maple-Brined Breast, 130
    H.T. Granola, 35
    Maple Baked Beans, 146
    Maple BBQ Rub, 166
    Maple-Marinated Leg of Lamb with Rosemary- and Garlic-Herbed Potatoes, 106
    Maple-Pecan Vinaigrette, 177

    Maple-Soy Marinade, 168
    Maple-Stout Marinade, 167
    Maple Stout-Marinated Beef Brisket, 116
    Maple Thyme-Glazed Salmon, 98
    Maple Wet Brine, 165
    Pecan Pie Filling, 199
    Roasted Beet Salad with Chèvre, Arugula, and Blood Orange Vinaigrette, 59
    Roasted Turkey, 127
Maple Baked Beans, 146
Maple BBQ Rub, 166
Maple-Marinated Leg of Lamb with Rosemary- and Garlic-Herbed Potatoes, 106
Maple-Pecan Vinaigrette, 177
Maple-Soy Marinade, 168
Maple-Stout Marinade, 167
Maple Stout-Marinated Beef Brisket, 116
Maple Thyme-Glazed Salmon, 98
Maple Wet Brine, 165
    Duck Confit and Maple-Brined Breast, 130
Marinades, 167–170
    Honey-Molasses Marinade, 170
    Maple-Soy Marinade, 168
    Maple-Stout Marinade, 167
    Mushroom Marinade, 170
Massachusetts Oysters, Preserved Lemon Maine Vodka and Horseradish, 76
Meat, 103–121
    BBQ Grilled and Braised Lamb Shanks, 104
    Beef and Pork Chili, 119
    Chipotle Spiced Pork, 116
    Cider-Braised Pork, 115
    Creamed Chipped Beef on Buttermilk Biscuits, 41
    Elysian Fields Farm, 109
    Ham and Potato Casserole, 109
    Ham Hock and Heirloom Bean Soup, 54
    Ham Hock Stock, 164
    Maple-Marinated Leg of Lamb with Rosemary- and Garlic-Herbed Potatoes, 106
    Maple Stout-Marinated Beef Brisket, 116
    Meatloaf, 110
    Pale Ale-Braised Short Ribs, 103
    Pot Roast, 121
    Pulled Pork, 107
    Rack of Venison, 118
    Red Flannel Hash with Poached Eggs, 37
    River Rock Farm Sirloin and Spinach Salad, 112
    Scotch Eggs, 38
    Skillet Breakfast, 43
    Smoked and Grilled Pork Chops, 115
    Veal or Oxtail Stock, 164
    Venison Sausage with Smoked Bacon Sauerkraut, 110
Meatloaf, 110
Minted Iced Tea, 205
Misty Knoll Farm, 124
Molasses
    Anadama Bread, 196
    Gingerbread Cake and Fresh Cream, 190
    Hasty Indian Pudding, 187
    Honey-Molasses Marinade, 170
    H.T. Granola, 35
    Nana's Baked Beans, 147
    Pecan Pie Filling, 199
    Pig Gingersnap Cookies, 195
    Pulled Pork, 107
Mulled Cider, 205
Mushroom(s)
    Grilled Portobello with Vermont Blythedale Farm Brie and Walnut Vinaigrette, 83
    Grit Cakes with Mushrooms, 73
    Mushroom Ketchup, 154

Mushroom Ketchup, 154
Mushroom Marinade, 170
  Grilled Portobello with Vermont Blythedale Farm Brie and Walnut Vinaigrette, 83
Mussels Dijon, 94
Mustard
  Champagne-Lemon Herb Vinaigrette, 175
  Cheshire Garden, 40
  Chicken Mustard, 167
  Crab Cakes, 70
  Creamy Garlic Dressing, 172
  Grilled Chicken Salad with Walnuts and Grapes on a Bed of Romaine, 125
  Honey-Molasses Marinade, 170
  Maple-Stout Marinade, 167
  Maple-Thyme Glazed Salmon, 98
  Mussels Dijon, 94
  Mustard Pickles, 153
  Mustard Vinaigrette, 175
  Nana's Baked Beans, 147
  Salmon Burgers, 95
  Venison Sausage with Smoked Bacon Sauerkraut, 110
  Warm Bacon Vinaigrette, 174
Mustard Greens
  Wilted Greens, 144
Mustard Pickles, 153
Mustard Vinaigrette, 175
  Scotch Eggs, 38

N
Native Onion Soup, 55
Nectarine(s)
  Grilled Striped Bass with Warm Fruit Salad and Pea Tendrils, 101
Nesenkeag Co-op Farm, 16, 51
New England Cheese Board, 69
New England Lobster Bake, 91
New England Seasonal Table, 23
Nut(s)
  Grilled Chicken Salad with Walnuts and Grapes on a Bed of Romaine, 125
  H.T. Granola, 35
  Maple-Pecan Vinaigrette, 177
  Pecan Pie Filling, 199
  Spinach Salad with Goat Cheese and Spicy Pecans, 60
  Walnut Vinaigrette, 174

O
Olive(s)
  Spiced Olives, 66
  Tapenade Bread, 66
Onion(s)
  Apple Chutney, 156
  Beef and Pork Chili, 119
  Country Vegetable Soup, 48
  Creamed Onions, 141
  Finnan Haddie, 92
  Flageolet Bean Salad, 152
  Goat Cheese Polenta Cake, 148
  Grilled Chicken Salad with Walnuts and Grapes on a Bed of Romaine, 125
  Grilled Vegetables with Chèvre and Basil Oil, 31
  Mustard Pickles, 153
  Native Onion Soup, 55
  Succotash, 136
Orange(s)
  Baked Carrots, 143
  Blood Orange Vinaigrette, 178
  Citrus Vinaigrette, 171
  Cranberry Chutney, 156
  Dried Stone Fruit Relish, 155
  Grilled Chicken Breast with Apple Cider Reduction, 131

  Grilled Citrus- and Dill-Cured Sablefish, 88
  Grilled Striped Bass with Warm Fruit Salad and Pea Tendrils, 101
  Mulled Cider, 205
  Roasted Beet Salad with Chèvre, Arugula, and Blood Orange Vinaigrette, 59
  Sangria, 202
  Spiced Olives, 66
Oven-Roasted Root Vegetables, 137
Oxtail Stock (or Veal Stock), 164
Oyster(s)
  Massachusetts Oysters, Preserved Lemon Maine Vodka and Horseradish, 76
  Woodbury's Seafood, 96

P
Pale Ale-Braised Short Ribs, 103
Pancakes (see Hotcakes)
Parsnip(s)
  Oven-Roasted Root Vegetables, 137
  Red Flannel Hash with Poached Eggs, 37
Pasta
  Chicken Noodle Soup, 46
  Macaroni and Cheese, 145
Pastrami
  Duck Pastrami, 70
Pastrami Rub, 166
Pastry
  Baked Stuffed Apple, 182
  Henrietta's Table Chicken Potpie, 123
  H.T. Daily Pie, 197
Pâté
  Bluefish Pâté, 67
Pea(s)
  Henrietta's Table Chicken Potpie, 123
Peach(es)
  Grilled Striped Bass with Warm Fruit Salad and Pea Tendrils, 101
Pearl Onion(s)
  Creamed Onions, 141
  Henrietta's Table Chicken Potpie, 123
Pea Tendrils
  Grilled Striped Bass with Warm Fruit Salad and Pea Tendrils, 101
Pecan(s)
  Maple-Pecan Vinaigrette, 177
  Pecan Pie Filling, 199
  Spinach Salad with Goat Cheese and Spicy Pecans, 60
Pecan Pie Filling, 199
Pepper(s)
  Beef and Pork Chili, 119
  Duck Hash, 32
  Flageolet Bean Salad, 152
  Kosher Dill Pickles, 151
  Pulled Pork, 107
  Romaine Salad with Creamy Garlic Dressing, 62
Pickle(s)
  Kosher Dill Pickles, 151
  Mustard Pickles, 153
  Pickled Apples, 150
  Tartar Sauce, 160
Pickled Apples, 150
Pies
  Apple Pie Filling, 198
  Butternut Squash Pie, 41
  Henrietta's Table Chicken Potpie, 123
  H.T. Daily Pie, 197
  Pecan Pie Filling, 199
  Pumpkin Pie Filling, 199
Pig Gingersnap Cookies, 195
Pizza of Maine Rock Crab, Dulse, and Sea Salt, 100
Plum(s)
  Grilled Striped Bass with Warm Fruit Salad and Pea Tendrils, 101
  Hot Smoked Bluefish with Beach Plum Vinaigrette, 97

Poached Salmon Roll, 92
Poached Salmon with Cucumber Dill Crème Fraîche, 36
Polenta
    Goat Cheese Polenta Cake, 148
    Grit Cakes with Mushrooms, 73
Pop's Bloody Mary Mix, 207
Pork
    Beef and Pork Chili, 119
    Chipotle Spiced Pork, 116
    Cider-Braised Pork, 115
    Pulled Pork, 107
    Smoked and Grilled Pork Chops, 115
Potato(es)
    Blue Cheese au Gratin Potatoes, 149
    Celery Root Potatoes, 148
    Duck Hash, 32
    Ham and Potato Casserole, 109
    Henrietta's Table Mashed Potatoes, 146
    Maple-Marinated Leg of Lamb with Rosemary- and Garlic-Herbed
        Potatoes, 106
    New England Lobster Bake, 91
    Skillet Breakfast, 43
Potpie
    Henrietta's Table Chicken Potpie, 123
Pot Roast, 121
Poultry, 123-132
    Chicken 2 Ways, 128
    Chicken Demi-glace, 168
    Chicken Noodle Soup, 46
    Chicken Stock, 163
    Duck Confit and Maple-Brined Breast, 130
    Duck Hash, 32
    Duck Pastrami, 70
    Grilled Chicken Breast with Apple Cider Reduction, 131
    Grilled Chicken Salad with Walnuts and Grapes on a Bed of
        Romaine, 125
    Henrietta's Table Chicken Potpie, 123
    Herb-Crusted Rotisserie Chicken, 132
    Jurgielwicz Farm, 132
    Misty Knoll Farm, 124
    Roasted Turkey, 127
Preserved Lemons, 158
    Grilled Native Asparagus, Feta, and EVOO, 78
    Massachusetts Oysters, Preserved Lemon Maine Vodka and
        Horseradish, 76
Preserves
    Cheshire Garden, 40
Prune(s)
    Dried Stone Fruit Relish, 155
Pudding
    Hasty Indian Pudding, 187
    Henrietta's Table Chocolate Bread Pudding with Cognac
        Caramelized Bananas, 201
    Winter Berry Pudding, 192
Pulled Pork, 107
Pumpkin(s)
    Fresh Pumpkin Whoopie Pies, 184
    Pumpkin Bread, 188
    Pumpkin Pie Filling, 199
    Roasted Pumpkin Soup, 49
    Sugar Pumpkin Slaw, 150
Pumpkin Bread, 188

R
Rack of Venison, 118
Ramps
    Grilled Striped Bass with Warm Fruit Salad and Pea Tendrils, 101
Raspberries
    Angelini Farming Trust, 159
    Cheshire Garden, 40
    Raspberry Lemonade, 204

    Sangria, 202
    Vanilla Cheesecake and Native Fresh Berry Compote, 191
    Winter Berry Pudding, 192
Red Flannel Hash with Poached Eggs, 37
Red Wine Sauce, 162
Relishes
    Dry Stone Fruit Relish, 155
Rhubarb
    Baked Strawberry Rhubarb French Toast, 29
    Strawberry Rhubarb Compote, 158
Ribs
    Pale Ale-Braised Short Ribs, 103
River Rock Farm, 112, 117
River Rock Farm Sirloin and Spinach Salad, 112
Roasted Beets, 143
**Roasted Beet Salad with Chèvre, Arugula, and Blood
    Orange Vinaigrette, 59**
Roasted Corn and Crab Chowder, 46
Roasted Pumpkin Soup, 49
Roasted Spicy Apples, 152
Roasted Turkey, 127
Rock Crab (see Crab)
Romaine
    Grilled Chicken Salad with Walnuts and Grapes on a Bed of
        Romaine, 125
    Romaine Salad with Creamy Garlic Dressing, 62
Romaine Salad with Creamy Garlic Dressing, 62
Root Vegetable(s)
    Baked Carrots, 143
    Blue Cheese au Gratin Potatoes, 149
    Nesenkeag Co-op Farm, 16, 51
    Oven-Roasted Root Vegetables, 137
    Red Flannel Hash with Poached Eggs, 37
Rotisserie
    Herb-Crusted Rotisserie Chicken, 132
Rubs
    Dry BBQ Rub, 166
    Maple BBQ Rub, 166
    Pastrami Rub, 166
Rum
    Baked Stuffed Apple, 182
    Dried Stone Fruit Relish, 155
    Pecan Pie Filling, 199
    Sangria, 202
Rutabaga(s)
    Oven-Roasted Root Vegetables, 137
    Red Flannel Hash with Poached Eggs, 37

S
Salads, 56-63
    Farmer's Cheese Salad, 63
    Flageolet Bean Salad, 152
    Grilled Chicken Salad with Walnuts and Grapes on a Bed of
        Romaine, 125
    Grilled Striped Bass with Warm Fruit Salad and Pea Tendrils, 101
    Iceberg Lettuce with Creamy Massachusetts Blue Cheese Dressing, 56
    River Rock Farm Sirloin and Spinach Salad, 112
    Roasted Beet Salad with Chèvre, Arugula, and Blood Orange
        Vinaigrette, 59
    Romaine Salad with Creamy Garlic Dressing, 62
    Spinach Salad with Goat Cheese and Spicy Pecans, 60
Salad Dressings (see dressings)
Salmon
    Homemade Smoked Salmon, 81
    Maple Thyme-Glazed Salmon, 98
    Poached Salmon Roll, 92
    Poached Salmon with Cucumber Dill Crème Fraîche, 36
    Salmon Burgers, 95
Salt Pork
    Maple Baked Beans, 146
    Nana's Baked Beans, 147

Sandwiches
    Cornmeal-Crusted Monkfish Sandwich, 87
Sangria, 202
Sauces, 160-162
    Applesauce, 160
    Bourbon BBQ Sauce, 162
    Cheshire Garden, 40
    Red Wine Sauce, 162
    Tartar Sauce, 160
    Tomato Basil Sauce, 161
Sauerkraut
    Venison Sausage with Smoked Bacon Sauerkraut, 110
Sausage
    Scotch Eggs, 38
    Skillet Breakfast, 43
    Venison Sausage with Smoked Bacon Sauerkraut, 110
Scallop(s)
    Smoked Scallop Chowder, 50
    Smoked Scallops, 80
Scrod, 98
Seafood, 87-101
    Bluefish Pâté, 67
    Cod Fish Cakes, 74
    Cornmeal-Crusted Monkfish Sandwich, 87
    Crab Cakes, 70
    Finnan Haddie, 92
    Grilled Citrus- and Dill-Cured Sablefish, 88
    Grilled Striped Bass with Warm Fruit Salad and Pea Tendrils, 101
    Homemade Smoked Salmon, 81
    Hot Smoked Bluefish with Beach Plum Vinaigrette, 97
    Lobster Chowder, 53
    Maple Thyme-Glazed Salmon, 98
    Massachusetts Oysters, Preserved Lemon Maine Vodka and
        Horseradish, 76
    Mussels Dijon, 94
    New England Lobster Bake, 91
    Pizza of Maine Rock Crab, Dulse, and Sea Salt, 100
    Poached Salmon Roll, 92
    Poached Salmon with Cucumber Dill Crème Fraîche, 36
    Roasted Corn and Crab Chowder, 46
    Salmon Burgers, 95
    Scrod, 98
    Smoked Scallop Chowder, 50
    Smoked Scallops, 80
    Woodbury's Seafood, 96
Seaweed
    New England Lobster Bake, 91
    Pizza of Maine Rock Crab, Dulse, and Sea Salt, 100
    Smoked Scallop Chowder, 50
Sherry
    Grit Cakes with Mushrooms, 73
    Lobster Chowder, 53
    Native Onion Soup, 55
Short Ribs
    Pale Ale-Braised Short Ribs, 103
Sides, 136-153
    Baked Carrots, 143
    Blue Cheese au Gratin Potatoes, 149
    Brussels Sprouts, 140
    Buttermilk Biscuits, 149
    Butternut Squash Puree, 144
    Caramelized Cauliflower, 142
    Celery Root Potatoes, 148
    Creamed Onions, 141
    Flageolet Bean Salad, 152
    Goat Cheese Polenta Cake, 148
    Grilled Asparagus, 136
    Henrietta's Table Mashed Potatoes, 146
    Kosher Dill Pickles, 151
    Macaroni and Cheese, 145
    Maple Baked Beans, 146

    Mustard Pickles, 153
    Nana's Baked Beans, 147
    Oven-Roasted Root Vegetables, 137
    Pickled Apples, 150
    Roasted Beets, 143
    Roasted Spicy Apples, 152
    Succotash, 136
    Sugar Pumpkin Slaw, 150
    Wilted Greens, 144
    Wilted Spinach, 138
Skillet Breakfast, 43
Slaw
    Sugar Pumpkin Slaw, 150
Smoked and Grilled Pork Chops, 115
    Applesauce, 160
Smoked Scallop Chowder, 50
Smoked Scallops, 80
Smoked Tomato Ketchup, 155
Smoothie
    Mixed Berry Smoothie, 202
Soups, 46-55
    Chicken Noodle Soup, 46
    Country Vegetable Soup, 48
    Ham Hock and Heirloom Bean Soup, 54
    Lobster Chowder, 53
    Native Onion Soup, 55
    Roasted Corn and Crab Chowder, 46
    Roasted Pumpkin Soup, 49
    Smoked Scallop Chowder, 50
Spiced Olives, 66
Spinach
    Country Vegetable Soup, 48
    River Rock Farm Sirloin and Spinach Salad, 112
    Spinach Salad with Goat Cheese and Spicy Pecans, 60
    Wilted Greens, 144
    Wilted Spinach, 138
Squash(es)
    Butternut Squash Pie, 41
    Butternut Squash Puree, 144
    Country Vegetable Soup, 48
    Grilled Vegetables with Chèvre and Basil Oil, 31
Starters, 66-83
    Bluefish Pâté, 67
    Cod Fish Cakes, 74
    Crab Cakes, 70
    Duck Pastrami, 70
    Grilled Native Asparagus, Feta, and EVOO, 78
    Grilled Portobello with Vermont Blythedale Farm Brie and Walnut
        Vinaigrette, 83
    Grit Cakes with Mushrooms, 73
    Homemade Smoked Salmon, 81
    Massachusetts Oysters, Preserved Lemon Maine Vodka and
        Horseradish, 76
    Smoked Scallops, 80
    Spiced Olives, 66
    Tapenade Bread, 66
Steak
    River Rock Farm, 112, 117
    River Rock Farm Sirloin and Spinach Salad, 112
Steamer Clams
    New England Lobster Bake, 91
Stocks, 163-164
    Chicken Stock, 163
    Ham Hock Stock, 164
    Veal or Oxtail Stock, 164
Stout
    Maple-Stout Marinade, 167
    Maple Stout-Marinated Beef Brisket, 116
Strawberries
    Baked Strawberry Rhubarb French Toast, 29
    Cheshire Garden, 40

Sangria, 202
Strawberry Rhubarb Compote, 158
Vanilla Cheesecake and Native Fresh Berry Compote, 191
Verrill Farm, 16, 169
Winter Berry Pudding, 192
Strawberry Rhubarb Compote, 158
Striped Bass
Grilled Striped Bass with Warm Fruit Salad and Pea Tendrils, 101
Succotash, 136
Sugar Pumpkin Slaw, 150
Swiss Chard
Wilted Greens, 144

T
Tapenade Bread, 66
Tartar Sauce, 160
Cornmeal-Crusted Monkfish Sandwich, 87
Crab Cakes, 70
Salmon Burgers, 95
Tea
Minted Iced Tea, 205
Tequila
Grilled Striped Bass with Warm Fruit Salad and Pea Tendrils, 101
Thyme
Maple Thyme-Glazed Salmon, 98
Tomato(es)
Apricot and Tomato Chutney, 157
Beef and Pork Chili, 119
Country Vegetable Soup, 48
Flageolet Bean Salad, 152
Grilled Vegetables with Chèvre and Basil Oil, 31
Grit Cakes with Mushrooms, 73
Iceberg Lettuce with Creamy Massachusetts Blue Cheese Dressing, 56
Mushroom Ketchup, 154
Pizza of Maine Rock Crab, Dulse, and Sea Salt, 100
Pop's Bloody Mary Mix, 207
Pulled Pork, 107
Smoked Tomato Ketchup, 155
Tapenade Bread, 66
Tomato Basil Sauce, 161
Verrill Farm, 16, 169
Tomato Basil Sauce, 161
Turkey
Misty Knoll Farm, 124
Roasted Turkey, 127
Turnip(s)
Oven-Roasted Root Vegetables, 137
Red Flannel Hash with Poached Eggs, 37

V
Vanilla Cheesecake and Native Fresh Berry Compote, 191
Veal
Veal Stock (or Oxtail Stock), 164
Vegetable(s)
Apricot and Tomato Chutney, 157
Baked Carrots, 143
Brussels Sprouts, 140
Butternut Squash Pie, 41
Butternut Squash Puree, 144
Caramelized Cauliflower, 142
Celery Root Potatoes, 148
Country Vegetable Soup, 48
Creamed Onions, 141
Flageolet Bean Salad, 152
Grilled Asparagus, 136
Grilled Native Asparagus, Feta, and EVOO, 78
Grilled Portobello with Vermont Blythedale Farm Brie and Walnut Vinaigrette, 83
Grilled Vegetables with Chèvre and Basil Oil, 31
Ham Hock and Heirloom Bean Soup, 54
Mushroom Ketchup, 154

Nesenkeag Co-op Farm, 16, 51
Oven-Roasted Root Vegetables, 137
Roasted Beets, 143
Smoked Tomato Ketchup, 155
Succotash, 136
Tomato Basil Sauce, 161
Wilted Greens, 144
Wilted Spinach, 138
Venison
Rack of Venison, 118
Venison Sausage with Smoked Bacon Sauerkraut, 110
Venison Sausage with Smoked Bacon Sauerkraut, 110
Verrill Farm, 16, 169
Vinaigrettes (see Dressings)
Vodka
Massachusetts Oysters, Preserved Lemon Maine Vodka and Horseradish, 76
Pop's Bloody Mary Mix, 207

W
Walnut(s)
Grilled Chicken Salad with Walnuts and Grapes on a Bed of Romaine, 125
Grilled Portobello with Vermont Blythedale Farm Brie and Walnut Vinaigrette, 83
Roasted Beet Salad with Chèvre, Arugula, and Blood Orange Vinaigrette, 59
Walnut Vinaigrette, 174
Walnut Vinaigrette, 174
Grilled Portobello with Vermont Blythedale Farm Brie and Walnut Vinaigrette, 83
Warm Bacon Vinaigrette, 174
Westfield Farm, 57, 69
Wet Brine, 165
Cider-Braised Pork, 115
Duck Pastrami, 70
Roasted Turkey, 127
Smoked and Grilled Pork Chops, 115
Wheat Berries
Smoked Scallop Chowder, 50
Whole Wheat Hotcakes, 30
Wilted Greens, 144
Wilted Spinach, 138
Wilting Greens
Ham Hock and Heirloom Bean Soup, 54
Wine
Chicken 2 Ways, 128
Chicken Demi-glace, 168
Fondue, 33
Lobster Chowder, 53
Mussels Dijon, 94
Pot Roast, 121
Rack of Venison, 118
Red Wine Sauce, 162
Sangria, 202
Smoked Scallop Chowder, 50
Tomato Basil Sauce, 161
Winter Berry Pudding, 192
Woodbury's Seafood, 96

Y
Yogurt
Farmer's Custard, 195
Mixed Berry Smoothie, 202

Z
Zucchini
Country Vegetable Soup, 48
Grilled Vegetables with Chèvre and Basil Oil, 31